Proofreading and Editing

Grade 7

Published by Milestone
an imprint of
Frank Schaffer Publications®

Editor: Lindsey Lautenbach
Interior Designer: Megan Grimm

Frank Schaffer Publications®

Milestone is an imprint of Frank Schaffer Publications.

Send all inquiries to:
Frank Schaffer Publications
3195 Wilson Drive NW
Grand Rapids, Michigan 49544

Proofreading and Editing—grade 7

ISBN: 0-7696-4057-5

1 2 3 4 5 6 7 8 9 10 PAT 10 09 08 07 06 05

Table of Contents

Proofreading Marks:

Introduction

On Your Mark

You will use special marks when you edit and proofread text. **Proofreading marks** show where and how to fix mistakes. They are clear and easy to use. These are the most common proofreading marks.

Proofreading mark	Meaning of mark	Corrected text
california ≡	make capital	California
Alice/in Wonderland	make lower case	Alice in Wonderland
What is ~~is~~ it?	delete text	What is it?
wolves	switch (transpose) the order	wolves
snow man	close space	snowman
Mrs Adams ^	insert	Mrs. Adams

Name _____   Date _____

Scoundrels on the Seas

Read each sentence below. Use one of the proofreading marks on page 4 to correct the mistake in each sentence. The hint at the end of the sentence will help you find the mistake.

1. Real pirates of the seven teenth century were not like the ones we see in today's movies.

    Hint: close space

2. Not all of them were mercilesss cutthroats.

    Hint: omit a letter

3. Captain tew, for example, was known for his kind treatment of prisoners.

    Hint: capitalize a letter

4. Many ships' Captains surrendered to him without any fight at all.

    Hint: make a letter lowercase

5. Another pirate, Captian Mission of France, even started a retirement home for old pirates.

    Hint: switch the order of two letters

6. However some pirates were feared for their harsh treatment of prisoners.

    Hint: insert a comma

7. A pirate named Stede Bonnet joined blackbeard, a ferocious pirate.

    Hint: capitalize a letter

8. Bonnet made his victims walk the Plank.

    Hint: make a letter lowercase

9. One of the the most famous pirates was Captain Kidd.

    Hint: omit a word

10. He started out as a privateer; captain who had permission from Great Britain to attack enemy ships.

    Hint: insert a word

Capitalization:

Sentences

Aliens and New Worlds

Read each sentence below. Use the correct proofreading mark to indicate which letters should be capitalized. On the line provided, write the number of the reason the letter should be capitalized.

- 1—first word of a sentence

- 2—proper noun

- 3—part of a book title

1. Edgar rice Burroughs wrote science fiction. _____

2. he is probably better known for his Tarzan series. _____

3. The books by George Orwell, *Animal farm* and *1984*, deal with serious social issues. _____

4. *Brave New World* by Aldous Huxley, a british novelist, describes a futuristic utopia. _____

5. Now a well-loved author, madeleine L'Engle, wrote *A Wrinkle in Time*, which was rejected by 20 publishers before it was accepted. _____

6. The book *Strangers in a Strange Land* by Robert Heinlein is about a human being who was raised by martians. _____

7. Best known for his novel about book burning, *Fahrenheit 451*, Ray Bradbury also wrote *The Martian Chronicles*, about the colonization of mars. _____

8. some science-fiction writers are true scientists, such as Isaac Asimov, who wrote *The Foundation Trilogy*. _____

9. Ursula Le guin authored both *Planet of Exile* and *Dispossessed*, both award-winning novels. _____

10. H. G. Wells' famous *The war of the Worlds* created quite a stir when a version of it was broadcasted on the radio in 1938. _____

Name _____   Date _____

War Presidents

Remember, use the ≡ mark to capitalize a letter, and use ℓc to make a letter lowercase.

Names of people, places, and pets are always capitalized.

James Buchanan was born in Cove Gap, Pennsylvania.

People's titles are capitalized only when the title goes in front of the name.

British Foreign Minister James Buchanan became president in 1857.

Do not capitalize a title that comes after a person's name.

James Buchanan was a president who was unable to prevent the Civil War.

Name of events are capitalized.

The Civil War would create many changes for the country.

Read the following sentences. Use proofreading marks to correct the capitalization.

1. When president Abraham lincoln took office, the country was ready for war.

2. abraham Lincoln was a President that believed in peace across the United states.

3. During his four short years in office, the President guided the country through the civil War until the Southern general Robert lee surrendered in 1865.

4. Only fifty years later, President Woodrow Wilson stated that "the world must be safe for democracy" as he led the United States in World war I.

5. The United States had only twenty years of peace before franklin roosevelt was president and led the country through another World War in 1941.

Choose the phrase with the correct capitalization.

6. _____

   a. Rutherford Hayes was just one President who helped to bring all the states together again after the Civil war.

   b. Rutherford hayes was just one president who helped to bring all the states together again after the Civil War.

   c. Rutherford Hayes was just one president who helped to bring all the states together again after the Civil War.

Capitalization:

Proper Nouns

War Presidents (cont.)

7. _____

    a. In 1963, Vice-President Lyndon Johnson took over the presidency after the assassination of President John F. Kennedy.

    b. In 1963, Vice-president Lyndon Johnson took over the Presidency after the assassination of President John f. Kennedy.

    c. In 1963, Vice-President Lyndon Johnson took over the presidency after the assassination of president John f. Kennedy.

8. _____

    a. President Johnson had a lot of decisions to make about the Vietnam war, which was causing much for the country.

    b. President Johnson had a lot of decisions to make about the Vietnam War, which was causing much sorrow for the Country.

    c. President Johnson had a lot of decisions to make about the Vietnam War, which was causing much sorrow for the country.

9. _____

    a. Just ten years earlier, President Dwight Eisenhower had ended a war against north Korea by bringing the United States troops home.

    b. Just ten years earlier, president Dwight Eisenhower had ended a War against North Korea by bringing the United States Troops home.

    c. Just ten years earlier, President Dwight Eisenhower had ended a war against North Korea by bringing the United States troops home.

10. _____

    a. In 1990, President George Bush led worldwide forces against Iraq in the Persian Gulf War.

    b. In 1990, president George Bush led worldwide forces against Iraq in the Persian gulf war.

    c. In 1990, President George Bush led Worldwide Forces against Iraq in the Persian Gulf War.

Name _____   Date _____

Sunken History

Capitalization:

Proper Nouns

Always capitalize the first word of a sentence. Also, words are usually capitalized when they stand for specific things, specific places, or specific people. Remember, the proofreading mark for capitalizing a letter is ≡ .

Specific things: months, titles of books, buildings, holidays, weekdays, heavenly bodies, events, languages, and trade names

Specific places: countries, states, cities, rivers, areas, parks, and postal abbreviations

Specific people: the pronoun I, proper names, title with a name, and nationalities

Use the proofreading mark to identify each letter to be capitalized in the paragraphs below.

lying on the bottom of lake superior under 530 feet of cold water is the edmund fitzgerald, a freighter that hauled iron and taconite ore from the western side of the great lakes to the steel factories in detroit, michigan. on november 10, 1975, the ship vanished during one of the area's most violent storms. all 29 crewmembers' bodies remain inside, entombed and undisturbed.

many ships have sunk to the murky bottoms of lakes because of harsh storms, but none have left behind as many questions as the wreck of the *edmund fitzgerald*. the freighter had left the port in superior, wisconsin, slightly ahead of the *arthur m. anderson*. suddenly a storm produced high waves and gale-force winds, but the two ships maintained close contact. at one point the *edmund fitzgerald* began to take on water, and the captain contacted the other ship with that information. a little while later, a snow squall destroyed visibility— both on the lake and on the radar screen. a final radio message from the *edmund fitzgerald* was heard: "we are holding our own." It was the last contact ever made. The ship disappeared from the surface of the water.

in the summer of 1994, nearly twenty years after the ship's disappearance, a team of scientists spent three days in an exploratory mini-submarine near the bottom of lake superior. they found the *edmund fitzgerald* and videotaped the ruins. the ship's 200-pound bronze bell was recovered on july 4, 1995. The bell is now on display in the great lakes shipwreck museum as a memorial to her lost crew.

0-7696-4057-5 *Proofreading and Editing*

Punctuation: ⌐

A Space Station Mission

End Marks ⌐

All sentences must end with a particular type of punctuation; an end mark.

A statement ends with a **period.** (.)

I've always wanted to live and work on a
space station.

A question should always end with a **question mark.** (?)

Have you ever considered pursuing such a goal?

An exclamatory sentence should end with an **exclamation mark.** (!)

It could be an amazing experience!

A command can end either with a period or an exclamation mark, depending on
the intensity of the speaker's feelings.

Be prepared for anything!

Try not to pack too much.

This is the proofreading mark to use to add punctuation: ∧
This is the proofreading mark to delete incorrect punctuation: ⌐

**Mark the following sentences about a space station mission, adding missing
end marks where necessary.**

1. My friends and I were chosen to work on the space station
2. We wondered what it would be like up there
3. What was our mission to be
4. Suddenly, we saw an asteroid coming our way
5. Fortunately, we were able to change our path
6. Always be aware of what's happening on the space station

**Proofread this paragraph about the space station, using the delete mark ⌐ to
remove incorrect punctuation, and the insert mark ∧ to add it where necessary.**

"How was your trip!" asked the Captain "Fine" we replied There was much work
to be done I wondered if we would start to feel homesick? "Don't worry" said
the Captain calmly! "You'll love it here"

Winter Vacation

Punctuation:

Commas

Commas are a form of punctuation we use to make clear to the reader all the separate ideas in a sentence. Editors must check to make sure commas are used correctly. To insert a comma use the ⌄ mark.

Commas go after prepositional phrases.

　　In the winter, I'm always waiting for snow.

Commas go between cities and states or countries.

　　There has been a large amount of snow this year in Minneapolis, Minnesota.

Commas go between words in a series.

　　Winter is a great time for outdoor sports like skiing, skating, and sledding.

Commas go after certain introduction words at the beginning of sentences.

　　Fortunately, my friends and I are able to do all these fun activities.

Read the rest of the story below. Use editing marks to insert commas in the appropriate places.

　　We were in school but not in school. That is to say our bodies were at our desks but our minds had traveled ahead to Friday. Friday was the last day of school before vacation. We stared out the window at the gray sky sending all of our energy to the clouds. "Snow!" we commanded them. "Snow please snow!"

　　At home there were lots of secret conversations. Mom whispering to our big sister. Dad whispering on the phone to Grandma. We could also hear the rustling of wrapping paper coming from the home office. We knew there were packages somewhere in the house but my brother and I could not find them. So we sat in the living room watching one silly holiday special after another. Out in the kitchen pies were baking. Cookies were baking. The scents of vanilla and almonds tormented us. But everything was for Saturday when the grandparents aunts uncles and cousins would start arriving. I munched gloomily on some salty pretzels instead.

　　On Friday we had a holiday party in class. It was a relief to get up and move around. The classroom was decorated with giant snowflakes and white crêpe paper. This was ironic because there was still no snow. I hovered near the windows sipping my tart red punch and glancing outside. I pressed my hand against the windowpane. It felt cold enough to snow. Why wasn't it snowing?

　　The last bell sounded both shrill and sweet. We bolted into the hallways. My brother and I met up at the stairs. We charged down the green stairwell down the brown-tiled lobby and onto the front steps of the school. We stood there for a moment. Lazy white flakes were drifting down from the sky. The grass was already wearing a white disguise.

Punctuation:

Semicolons and Colons

Performing Well

Editors have to see that colons and semicolons are being used correctly in a piece of writing. Also, an editor may rewrite work to use colons or semicolons to make the writing more interesting.

Although colons and semi-colons look similar, they have very different uses.

A colon (:) is used to:

- Start a list of items.

  You need several things to perform well in class: a pen, a notebook, your textbook, and concentration!

- Let the reader know you are going to explain something.

  Let me tell you how to do well in this class: pay attention.

- Let the reader know you are about to define something, as in a dictionary. Concentration (noun): the ability to focus mentally.

A semi-colon (;) is used to:

- Connect two independent clauses. An independent clause is one that could be a complete sentence on its own. By joining two independent clauses with the semicolon, you are saying that there is some relationship between the ideas in the two independent clauses. The relationship could be a contrast or a cause and effect.

  I concentrate very well in class; some people do not.

  I never get to class late; I'm afraid I'll miss something important. (You don't need to use the word "because," if you use the semicolon here.)

- Show a change or transition.

  Janine does well in school; in addition, she works at a part time job.

  You should take your umbrella with you; otherwise, you might get wet.

Whatever the relationship the semicolon demonstrates, it allows the reader to think about what is happening, without being directly told. This also makes reading more interesting.

You can also use semicolons to separate things in a list where each item has more than one part to it:

We visited so many amazing cities on our cross-country trip: New York, New York; Philadelphia, Pennsylvania; Chicago, Illinois; and Los Angeles, California.

Performing Well (cont.)

Punctuation:

Semicolons and Colons

Read and edit the sentences below. Insert a colon or a semicolon where it is needed. Use the insert mark $\wedge$ to do this. Remove a semicolon or colon from a sentence where it does not belong. Use the delete mark to do this.

1. I rarely eat snacks on the couch: my mother doesn't like crumbs.

2. I'll tell you what I like for dessert ice cream.

3. I have to meet three teachers Mr. Green of the math department Ms. Holden of the history department and Mr. Trent of the science department.

4. Biology (noun); the study of living things.

5. Josh is a hardworking student however, he does have trouble with math.

6. Shelly wants to go to the art museum she has a great interest in painting.

Now look at these pairs of sentences. See if you can rewrite each pair as a single sentence, using colons or semicolons.

7. Ed wants to pursue lots of interests. These interests are biking, skating, and swimming.

   _____

8. I don't watch French movies without subtitles. This is because I don't know enough French yet to understand.

   _____

9. My brother's favorite sport is basketball. Baseball is the game I love.

   _____

10. There is one way to deal with this problem. Be honest.

   _____

0-7696-4057-5 *Proofreading and Editing*

Punctuation:

Quotation Marks

Family Tree

Quotation marks help to separate words that people actually said, from the rest of what the writer is telling you. Editors check to make sure quotation marks are used correctly. Use the ˅̎ to insert quotation marks.

"I want to find out more about our family," said Sonia to her mom.

Put quotation marks outside of a quote, or a person's words, and any punctuation that is a part of the person's words.

"What would you like to know?" her mom asked.

Capitalize the first word of the quote.

"I'd like to start with how Grandma and Grandpa met," said Sonia. "No one has ever told me that."

Use a comma, question mark, or exclamation point to divide the quotation from the rest of the sentence.

"What else would you like to find out about?" Sonia's mom asked.

Read the following story about researching a family tree. All the quotation marks have been left out. Use the insert quotations mark ˅̎ to show where they should be used. Remember, there should be a quotation mark at the beginning and ending of any statement that was spoken by a person in the story.

How did Grandma and Grandpa meet each other, Mom? asked Sonia.

I didn't know you were interested in that old stuff, her mother replied, smiling. They met in 1936. They helped out on the same farm after school. Grandma didn't have many friends at the time.

What were Grandma's mother and father named? asked Sonia.

Their names were Regina and Gerald Hellstern, said her mother. Gerald was the first person in his whole family to be born outside of Germany. That was in 1885. His family had been in the United States for four years when he was born.

Sonia was impressed. Wow, that was a long time ago. How do you know about all this?

For the past few years, your uncle and I have been researching our family history, her mother answered. We have reconstructed a family tree that goes all the way back to 1749.

It Adds Up

Punctuation:

Apostrophes

Editors must check to see that apostrophes are used correctly. There are two uses for apostrophes. One way apostrophes are used is to join two words, eliminating some of the letters. The apostrophe shows where the letters that were left out used to be. To add this punctuation, use the ⌄' mark.

To join the words *she* and *would*, you would write *she'd*. The apostrophe shows where the letters *woul* used to be.

Read the following sentences. Make sure the apostrophes are included correctly in the contraction, or combination words. Use proofreading marks to add apostrophes where needed.

1. Shell clean her room after she finishes studying for her test.

2. Hed do well on his project if he worked hard.

3. Hes much taller than her.

4. Im excited about the vacation.

5. Youre a fast reader.

Underline the contraction in each pair.

6. there, they're

7. where, we're

8. heed, he'd

0-7696-4057-5 *Proofreading and Editing*

Punctuation:

Apostrophes

Own It!

Apostrophes are also used to show possessives. Possessives show that someone owns something. Editors look to make sure possessives are used correctly. Both singular and plural nouns can be made possessive. Use the ✓ mark to add apostrophes.

That is Suzy's dog.

They didn't know what to buy for the twins' birthday present.

Some words are pluralized without adding an –s or –es.

In this case, add an 's.

women's

children's

Read the following sentences. Use proofreading marks to change the italicized phrases to their possessive forms. Then rewrite the sentences, using the possessive form.

1. It was *the idea of our teacher* to take a class hike.

   _____

2. The *observations of the students* were written down in the class journal.

   _____

3. Many liked studying the *reactions to humans of the forest animals*.

   _____

4. Others enjoyed looking at the *leaves and roots of the plant*.

   _____

5. Some decided that the *soil of the forest* was more interesting.

   _____

Read the following phrases. Write the possessive forms on the line.

6. wings of the bluebird

   _____

7. texture of the soil

   _____

8. legs of the beetle

   _____

Name _____   Date _____

Dog Data

Now use the information you've learned so far to edit these sentences about dogs. Remember to use the insert mark ∨ to add punctuation where it is needed, and the delete mark ⌐ to remove it where it's not correct.

1. Do you consider a dog your best friend.

2. It is good to know something about this species; that has lived with humans for thousands of years.

3. Some scientists believe that dogs are the animal cousins of wolves, with dogs and wolves sharing the same ancestor?

4. Unlike a wolfs bark a dogs bark is rather noisy.

5. When a dog barks, he is saying, I notice something unusual. Pay attention.

6. A barking dog wants one thing your attention.

7. The expression wolf down ones food comes from observing wolves quick eating habits.

Punctuation:

Using Italics

A Love of Theatre

Italics (typed letters that slant to the right) are used to make the reader pay attention to something in a sentence. You use *italics* to point out:

- Titles of complete or major works such as books, newspapers, magazines, movies, television shows, long poems, and plays that are at least three acts in length (titles of shorter works can be set off with quotation marks):

    One of Shakespeare's most famous plays is *Romeo and Juliet*.

    War and Peace is a famous Russian novel.

- Foreign words that have not become a part of English (as opposed to a phrase like "bon voyage"):

    Many people like pasta best when it is cooked *al dente*.

- Words that you are referring to as words themselves:

    There are too many *howevers* in this essay for my taste.

- Words or phrases that you wish to emphasize:

    The very *survival of our theatre* group depends on this fundraiser!

Italics should not be extended to include punctuation marks, such as end marks, or parentheses that are next to the words being italicized unless those punctuation marks are part of the thing or title that is being italicized:

"Have you seen the play *Macbeth?*" is not correct, but

"I just read the book *Where Have All the Flowers Gone?*" is correct.

You should not italicize the apostrophe –*s* in the possessive form of a title.

What does the *Washington Post*'s reporter say about the story?

Read the following story. Underline and use the proofreading mark for italics *ital* **to put words into italics where appropriate. Underline and use the proofreading mark for take out italics** *no ital* **to remove italics from words that should not be italicized.**

I have always loved the theatre. I suppose it started when my parents took me to see a production of Shakespeare's As You Like It. I love classic theatre, but I like modern *plays* as well. Did you see that new play Off the Wall? Its only one act, but it's very funny. It's based on the novel Upside Down. I read the review of it in the New York Times, and I knew I just *had to see it*.

In the Village

Punctuation:

Mixed Mechanics

Now it's time to practice the proofreading and editing skills you have learned so far. Read the following story about what an Incan farming village might have been like. All the punctuation has been removed, and words that should be italicized, have been put in regular print. Use proofreading symbols to correctly add punctuation and italics where necessary.

Have you ever wondered what a typical Incan farming village was like Picture this huge, snow-capped mountains tower over the small cluster of huts The small brown grass-roofed huts in the village are made out of dried mud called adobe

The sleeping village wakes early when the air flowing down from the mountains is still cold and blusters between the huts. Children go out to gather sticks to feed the fire but there are few trees so hunting for sticks is a challenge After a small meal some villagers take their goats and sheep out to graze while others go to work in the fields Corn potatoes peanuts and tomatoes are some of the main crops dotting the distant terraced fields

At midday the main meal is prepared A strong bitter scent drifts from the clay jugs of chicha a drink made from corn As the sun reaches down to the little village heavy woolen blankets as rough as dry grass are spread over stools or fences to dry and air out Excitement spreads through the village at the sight of a chasqui a messenger who is carrying news and information from the cities to the smaller villages They are happy to see him he is their only source of news

0-7696-4057-5 *Proofreading and Editing*

Spelling

Expert Spelling

A simple but important part of making sure a piece of writing is ready for the world, is checking that all words are spelled correctly. Editors need to have excellent, expert spelling skills, so that they can recognize it immediately when a writer makes an error in spelling. Of course, an expert speller also knows that if he or she is not sure about the spelling of a word, the best thing to do is look it up in the dictionary. When they find spelling errors, editors use the ⟿ mark to take out extra letters or to delete an entire word, and use the ∧ mark to insert the correct letters or word.

Below is a list of misspelled words. Can you write the correct spellings on the lines?

1. acess _____

2. estemate _____

3. feested _____

4. speek _____

5. terrable _____

6. gratest _____

7. generus _____

8. tabel _____

9. frie _____

10. goodby _____

11. independant _____

12. cooporation _____

13. biger _____

14. dirtey _____

15. pretence _____

Remarkable Rooms

Spelling

Sometimes it's hard to find a spelling error in the middle of a sentence, when you are being distracted by other things. Read the following story about unusual vacation lodgings. Look for the misspelled words and correct them using the proofreading symbols you have learned. Use the ⌒ℓ mark to take out extra letters or to delete an entire word, and use the ∧ mark to insert the correct letters or word.

You may find more comfortable surroundings, but it would be hard to find more unique overnite stays than in these four loonie lodgings. The first hotel on our tour is Jules's Undersea Lodge, named after Jules Verne who wrote *Twenty Thousand Leagues Under the Sea*. This two-room lodge is ancored to the floor of a lagoon in Key Largo, Florida. Once an underwater mobile research lab, it convertid into a hotel in 1986. Because its entrance can only be reached by scuba diving, guests can pack only the nesesities in one small, waterproof suitcase. The hotel acktualy has room service and its own chef.

If an underwater adventure doesn't apeal to you, try out the Ariau Jungle Hotel in Brazil. All of the 138 rooms in this spatious hotel are built on stilts and touch the treetops of the Amazon rainforest. One room sits atop a tree on the banks of the Rio Negro. It can be reeched only by boat. Guests can swim in a pool, play in a game room, or go on searches for alligators and piranas. In your room, monkeys swinging past your windows will entertane you. Be sure not to feed these treetop acrobats or your room will be overrun with them!

For the budget-minded, a Japanese capsal hotel is the place to go. These rooms resembel microwaves from the outside; a small door swings outward. The inside is only several feet wide and about six feet (1.8 meters) long. There's no room service, but you can buy food from vending mashines in the lobby.

The Ice Hotel in Jukkasiarvi, Sweden, is our last stop. It's made entireley of ice and snow. The rooms are not heated. Even the beds are made from snow, frozen into soled rectangles. For warmth, each guest is given reindeer skins and a sleeping bag. This frozen accommodation melts each spring and then is reconstructed every fall. You should plan on brining a coat, gloves, and a hat to this icy restaurant!

Spelling:

Plurals and Possessives

Family Reunion

The term **possessive** means the form of word that shows something belongs to something or someone. With a singular word, or a word that does not end in an *s*, this is shown by placing an **apostrophe** at the end of the word and adding an *s*.

This is Jennifer's address.

I can see Samir's house from here.

For plurals, or words that already end in *s*, you must add the apostrophe <u>after</u> the word (after the *s* at the end of the word).

All the houses' floor plans are identical.

The families' taste shows in their choice of paint colors.

If a plural word does not end in an *s*, then to make the possessive, add an apostrophe and an *s*.

The children's bedrooms are especially expressive.

Exception: When the word *it* shows possession, no apostrophe is used.

Though its floor plan is ordinary, the house is quite beautifully decorated.

Read the following story about a family reunion. Use the ∨ mark to add an apostrophe. Use the ⟩— mark to delete an apostrophe where it should not be.

1. My mom and all her siblings and cousins' have a big family reunion each year.

2. My aunts' kids are closest in age to me and my brother's, so we're glad when she brings them.

3. My mom's brother's wives are among my favorite people, and they bring great desserts!

4. The childrens' table at dinner has gotten a lot bigger over the years.

5. After a terrific, big dinner, the relative's appetites are taken care of, and its time for games!

6. My cousin's game skills are often better than mine, but they're all good sports.

7. My moms' mood is up for weeks after the reunion, since she loves to see her familys faces all together.

8. A reunion is a great thing for any family; all it's members get to have a special kind of fun!

Home Décor

A verb is a word that shows action or activity. An active verb shows someone or something doing something. A passive verb shows someone or something having something done to him, her or it. Generally, it's more interesting to read a piece of writing that has more active verbs. Editors check to make sure the writer uses as many active verbs as possible.

For example:

Passive: That room *was painted* for me by my friend Jeff.

Active: My friend Jeff *painted* that room for me.

Read the following story about decorating a house, and on a separate sheet of paper rewrite the sentences to make the verbs more active and less passive. Hint: when changing a verb form from passive to active, you often must change a pronoun form, too.

1. This entire house was decorated by me and my friends.

2. First, Jeff, me, and the others, were driven to the home improvement store by my friend, Jennifer.

3. The colors of the paint were chosen by me.

4. However, each of my friends was consulted by me, about which wallpaper to choose.

5. The supplies, and the new curtains and cushions were all brought back to the house by Steve.

6. The wallpaper was carefully applied to the walls by all of us.

7. It took hours for the furniture to be rearranged by me, Jeff, and Steve.

8. Finally, the garbage was picked up and the whole scene was cleaned up by the whole crowd.

9. It was a lot of work, but a great task was accomplished by all of us.

Subject-Verb Agreement:

Agreeing in Number

At the Zoo

The most important parts of a sentence are the subject and predicate. Every sentence must have a subject and a predicate to be a complete sentence. Verbs are the main part of a predicate. Editors must also know that a verb has to match the subject in several different ways. One way is in number.

Rules for present verbs:

If a subject is a singular noun or pronoun (he, she, it), add an *s* to the verb.

The ocean water *helps* to form hurricanes.

If a subject is I, you, or more than one person or thing, the verb should not end in an *s*.

Hurricanes *develop* over the ocean water.

This is generally the pattern for all regular (predictable) verbs. The pattern for all the forms of a verb in a tense is called a **conjugation**.

Here is an example of how to conjugate a regular verb *(to walk)* in the present tense:

I walk	we walk
you (singular) walk	you (plural) walk
he, she, or it walks	they walk

Some verbs are irregular, or do not follow the same patterns as most verbs. A common irregular verb is the verb *to be*. Here is a conjugation in the present tense for *to be*:

I am	Sentence: I am scared of hurricanes. (am)
you (singular) are	Sentence: Are you scared of hurricanes? (are)
he, she, or it is	Sentence: Even my father is scared of hurricanes. (is)
we are	Sentence: We are always drilled on hurricane procedure. (are)
you (plural) are	Sentence: She asked the class, "Are you prepared?" (are)
they are	Sentence: Are your friends scared of hurricanes? (are)

Since irregular verbs are unpredictable, you will have to recognize and memorize these verbs over time.

Name _____ Date _____

Surprise!

Another way that subjects need to fit with verbs is in tense, or time. All verbs have three major tenses: **present, past,** and **future.** This is how we are able to show the difference between events that happened yesterday, events that happen today, and those that will happen tomorrow.

Past verbs agree with subjects in a different way than present verbs. Most verbs are put in past tense by adding –*ed*.

Present: She *looks* at her.

Past: She looked at her.

If the past tense of a verb does not end in –*ed*, then it is an irregular verb. The verb *to be* is an irregular verb. Other examples are *to come, to make, to give,* and *to say*. Some past verbs have helping verbs in front of them, like the word *had*.

Read the past tense verbs below. Circle the number next to the verbs that are irregular.

1. was
2. let
3. climbed
4. walked
5. did
6. drove
7. began
8. studied
9. played
10. ate
11. said
12. were
13. rained
14. grated
15. sang

0-7696-4057-5 *Proofreading and Editing*

Subject-Verb Agreement:

Agreeing in Tense

Surprise! (cont.)

Read the following sentences. The underlined verb is incorrect. Write the correct form of the verb on the line. (Hint: it should be in past tense.)

16. Jenny remembered how it <u>happens</u>.

_____

17. Her mother <u>tells</u> her she had to do some errands before she could pick up Jenny.

_____

18. When her mother <u>is picking</u> her up, she seemed busy and rushed.

_____

19. Jenny <u>wonders</u> what was wrong.

_____

20. She asked her mother why she was so rushed, but her mother <u>says</u> she had forgotten to do something while she had been doing her chores.

_____

21. "Can we stop by grandmother's house?" her mother <u>asks</u>. "I need to drop something off."

_____

22. They <u>pulls</u> up to grandma's house, and her mother got out to pull the box from the back seat.

_____

23. "Can you help me carry this in?" Mother <u>says</u>.

_____

24. As they <u>struggling</u> to get the box in, Jenny heard noises coming from the living room.

_____

25. Suddenly, everyone came out of the living room and <u>screaming</u>, "Happy Birthday!"

_____

26. Jenny's mother <u>smiles</u> at her then. "Want to see what your cake looks like?" she said, pointing to the big box.

_____

Class Project

Grammar:

Pronouns and Antecedents

Editors must check to make sure that pronouns and antecedents all match correctly. A **pronoun** is a word you can substitute for a noun. An **antecedent** is the particular person, place, or thing (noun) that the pronoun refers to. Using pronouns makes writing better, when you don't want to use the name of something or someone too many times. For instance, decide which one of the following two sentences sounds better:

> I told Cheryl that Cheryl was the only person who had not done Cheryl's part of the class project, but Cheryl did not want to talk about not doing the class project.

> or

> I told Cheryl that she was the only person who had not done her part of the class project, but she did not want to talk about not doing it.

The pronoun *she* refers to Cheryl and the pronoun *it* refers to Cheryl's part of the project.

A pronoun must agree with its antecedent in three ways: person, (Is it first person: I, we? or second person: you? or third person: it, he, she, they?) number, (Is it singular: one entity? or plural: numerous entities?) and gender (Is it masculine? or feminine?).

> Incorrect: If a student wants to succeed in this class, you have to pay attention.

The noun *student* is a *he* or *she* but the pronoun used here is *you*. That does not match!

> Correct: If a student wants to succeed in this class, he or she has to pay attention.

Hint: Very often when someone is writing about a person, and it is not known if the person described is a boy or girl, the writer uses the pronoun "they".

> Our new teacher had not yet arrived and we did not know what they would be like.

This is not correct. If you know you are writing about a single person, you must use a singular pronoun. In this situation, you should write "he" or "he or she."

0-7696-4057-5 *Proofreading and Editing*

Grammar:

Pronouns and Antecedents

Class Project (cont.)

Read the following sentences about a group of students doing a class project. Proofread and correct the incorrectly used pronouns. Substitute pronouns for nouns where it would make the sentence better.

1. Our class decided to do a project together, because our class likes working together.

   _____

   _____

2. When many people cooperate on something, you usually get a great result.

   _____

   _____

3. My friend Mark suggested we do a video about the historical society in our town, and about the historical society's origins, because it interests Mark so much.

   _____

   _____

4. I heard that one of the students promised to bring in a video camera from home, but they couldn't bring the video camera, after all.

   _____

   _____

Class Project (cont.)

When the pronouns I and you are used, it's usually pretty easy to figure out which antecedent in a sentence they refer to. When third person pronouns (he, she, it, they) are used, and there is more than one noun in the sentence, it can sometimes be confusing to the reader. When a pronoun reference is unclear, it makes a sentence hard to read.

Both Jon and Nelson love his cooking.

Whose good cooking do they love? Jon's or Nelson's? There is no way to tell, so it is better not to use the pronoun in this situation.

Both Jon and Nelson love Nelson's cooking.

Read on about the class project. See if you can make confusing sentences easier to read. Fix any other problems you see in the sentences.

5. Jennelle wrote a script and so did Kayla, and we could see she was very talented.

   _____

   _____

6. Keith and Jay created a videotaping schedule, and made copies of the script, and he handed them out to all the students in the class.

   _____

   _____

7. Our teacher took us on many trips to the historical society, and we found the historical society to be a very interesting place.

   _____

   _____

8. The members of our class found out that its town had been founded by James Peterson, and Robert Stevens, and he was a very interesting person who invented several things.

   _____

   _____

Grammar:

School Uniforms

Pronoun Case

Pronoun Case means the way pronouns change when they are used for different things. Here are the three cases for pronouns:

1. Subjective case: This is when a pronoun is used as a subject.

    I drove to the store. (The word *I* is the subjective pronoun, the one doing the action.)

2. Objective case: This is when a pronoun is used as the object of a verb or preposition.

    John drove me to the store. (The word *me* is the objective pronoun.)

3. Possessive case: This is when the pronoun shows who or what possesses, or owns something.

    John drove us in his car. (The word *his* is the possessive pronoun.)

Below is a chart to help you keep track of the different forms of pronouns.

Hint: In the possessive case, the first pronoun listed works like an adjective, and the second pronoun works like a noun.

Pronoun Cases

Subjective	Objective	Possessive
I	Me	My, Mine
You	You	Your, Yours
He	Him	His
She	Her	Her, Hers
It	It	Its
We	Us	Our, Ours
They	Them	Their, Theirs

School Uniforms (cont.)

Grammar:

Pronoun Case

Read the following story about a mix-up with some school uniforms. Proofread for mistakes with the pronoun cases. Delete any incorrect pronouns. Insert the correct pronoun where it is needed.

1. In me school, we all wear school uniforms.

2. Ours uniform consists of a white shirt, a gray jacket, and blue pants, and everyone cleans our own uniform.

3. A funny thing happened recently to my friends and I on the boys' basketball team.

4. We visited the players at another school, to play basketball with us.

5. Our school bus driver was late in getting us there, because it couldn't find a route without traffic.

6. When we got to the locker room, the team and me had to change into their basketball uniforms very quickly.

7. They left our school uniforms all over the place; in fact, me friend William threw her jacket at I in a panic.

8. Ours team won, and they all felt pretty good.

9. But when we went back to the locker room, you could see we had a problem.

10. The school uniforms were scattered all over the floor; they was a mess.

11. Since the parts are identical, it wasn't easy for I and the others to figure out which parts belonged to each one of them.

12. Was this grey jacket my or his? Should I put on that shirt, or hand it to he?

13. It took a long while, but we finally sorted out the clothes, and each person had their own uniform back.

14. Of course, on the bus trip home, I found a note in its jacket pocket that said, "Remember to bring home yours science book," in someone else's handwriting.

15. I waved the note in the air, and William and me realized we had each others' jackets.

16. "Thanks a lot" said William glumly, "Now I have no excuse to forget bringing home your science book."

Grammar:

Who, That, or Which?

A Day at the Beach

The words *that*, *which*, and *who* each have different jobs. Editors check to make sure that the writer used the correct one of these words in a sentence.

The word *who* is used to talk about people. The word *that* is usually used to talk about things, but sometimes it may refer to a particular type of person. The word *which* is used to talk about things. It can also be used in the second idea of a sentence, to talk about the first idea in a sentence.

This is a notebook that I use for English class.

These are the clothes that I wear for gym.

She is the woman who will be teaching us writing.

It's raining today, which makes it hard to go swimming.

They are the kind of people who always forget their work. (It's OK to use the word that, because we are describing a certain type of people.)

Read the following story about a day at the beach. Proofread to see that the writer used the words *that*, *who*, and *which* correctly. Use the ⟋ mark to remove an incorrect word. Use the ∨ mark to add a word that is needed.

1. My friends and I are the kind of people which really like going to the beach.

2. It rained for ten days in a row, that meant we could not go to the beach.

3. One morning I woke up and saw it was the kind of day who was perfect for going to the beach.

4. It's Jenny's mom that always drives us to the beach when no one else can.

5. She's really the kind of person which likes to help out in a pinch.

6. After Jenny and her mom picked me up, it was Dennis that was to be picked up.

7. He had on a funny looking hat, who made us laugh.

8. "Laugh all you want," said Dennis, "but I'm the kind of person which burns easily."

9. We set up our things on the sand, and sat under a sun which was extremely hot.

10. It was a day who was filled with a lot of fun.

11. Of course, Dennis had the last laugh. By the time we went home, he was the only one which didn't have a sunburned face!

Name _____ Date _____

Contemplating Color

Editors must check to see that the writer used the correct form of an adjective. The **comparative** form of an adjective helps to compare two things. The **superlative** form of an adjective shows the "winner" in a comparison of a group of three or more people or things.

Adjective: She is a *tall* girl.

Comparative: This girl is *taller* than that one.

Superlative: That girl is the *tallest* of the three of them.

The word *than* often comes after a comparative word, and the word *the* often comes before a superlative word. Usually, to make an adjective into a comparative, add the ending *–er* and for the superlative add the ending *–est*.

We add *–ier* and *–iest* to change a two-syllable adjective that ends in a *y*, like happy. If an adjective has more than two syllables, we put the word *more* for the comparative, and *most* in front of the adjective, instead of changing the adjective itself (expensive, more expensive, most expensive).

There are also some adjectives that are irregular in the comparative and superlative forms:

Adjective: good, bad, far, little

Comparative: better, worse, further, less

Superlative: best, worst, furthest, least

Proofread to correct adjectives, comparatives, and superlatives that are used incorrectly.

1. It seems that blue is the calmer color of all of the colors in the rainbow.

2. Blue has often been chosen as the relaxingest color, symbolizing tranquility.

3. Red makes people feel exciteder than other colors do, since it increases heart rate and speeds up breathing.

4. For centuries, the color purple was the favorite of kings and queens. That was originally because purple dye was the most expensive, and only the richer of all people could afford it.

Grammar:

Misplaced Modifiers

Venice

A **modifier** is a word, phrase, or clause, which modifies (changes or describes) something else in a sentence. A **misplaced modifier** is one that has been put in the wrong place in the sentence. When this happens, it is not clear to the reader what the modifier is supposed to modify! An editor must recognize these confusing, misplaced modifiers, and put them in the right place. A modifying word should be near the words it modifies.

Misplaced: You will *only* need to buy one package of cake mix, to make this cake. (This would mean that buying the package of cake mix is the only thing you need to do at all for the cake to be made.)

Corrected: You will need to buy *only* one package of cake mix, to make this cake.

A modifying phrase should always be right next to the word it is modifying.

Incorrect: My uncle could be described as a thin man with a moustache weighing 150 pounds. (This makes it sound like the moustache weighs 150 pounds!)

Correct: My uncle could be described as a thin man weighing 150 pounds, with a moustache. (Now the man weighs 150 pounds.)

Incorrect: Though she is only five, my mother lets my sister set the table for dinner. (This makes it sound as though the mother is only five!)

Correct: Though my sister is only five, my mother lets her set the table.

Read the following sentences. Proofread and correct the misplaced modifiers.

1. Just before leaving on this trip, a television was delivered to our house.

2. A man drove it to our house to deliver it in a van.

3. Today, I watched a family bring home a new TV in Venice to their house in a very different way.

4. Living on a canal, the set had to be transported by rowboat.

5. Strangely beautiful, people live in Venice because the of city's wonderful surprises and canals.

6. The canals are full of *gondolas*, large canoes run by boat operators that serve as taxis.

7. Faster and more efficient, people also may travel on a *vaporetto*, which goes quickly from station to station.

8. Venice was first built on a series of 118 islands that filled the Lagoon of Venice 1,000 years ago.

One Negative Is Enough

Grammar:

Double Negatives

Editors must make a correction if an author uses a **double negative**. A double negative happens when you put two negative words in the same sentence. Usually, one negative word comes before the verb. Two negative words in one sentence makes the sentence mean the opposite of the idea intended. To make the meaning clear, use only one negative word in a sentence.

Incorrect: She is not going to buy no milk.

Correct: She is not going to buy milk. or She is not going to buy any milk.

Use proofreading marks to take out the extra negative word in the following sentences. If the sentence does not make sense after taking out the extra negative word, you may need to add a word like *any* or *anything* to make it complete.

1. She has not done no work.

2. Sandy did not worry about nothing when she left the park.

3. I don't have no homework, so I'm watching the movie.

4. My mom says she doesn't have no time to clean up the mess we made in the house.

5. He wants you to know that he didn't mean nothing by what he said to you.

6. I've looked around for your notebook, but I haven't found it nowhere.

7. Nobody never gets nothing done around here before lunch.

Name _____ Date _____

An editor must know about the correct structures of different kinds of sentences.

Sentences are made up of clauses. An **independent clause** has a main subject and a verb. It can be a complete sentence by itself. A **dependent clause** cannot stand alone as a sentence, because it does not have all the necessary parts of a sentence. It needs to be connected to an independent clause. There are names for different types of sentences. A **simple sentence** is made of one independent clause. It has a subject and a predicate (the part of the sentence which says something about the subject) and expresses a complete thought. A **compound sentence** has two independent clauses. These clauses are joined by a conjunction (and, but, or, for, nor, yet, so). A **complex sentence** also has two clauses. At least one has to be an independent clause, but the other can be a dependent clause. These clauses can be joined by a comma or a conjunction.

Read the following sentences. Write S for a simple sentence, C for a compound sentence, and CX for a complex sentence.

1. _____ Not thinking about the consequences, Benjamin Franklin flew a kite in a thunderstorm.

2. _____ He was only concentrating on his new experiment.

3. _____ A lightning bolt heats the air up to five times the heat of the surface of the sun, but the charge is so brief that people can often survive a lightning hit.

4. _____ The bolt that hit his kite was weak so Franklin was lucky.

5. _____ Through this experiment, Franklin proved that lightning is actually electricity.

6. _____ Franklin later invented the lightning rod.

Editors must make sure that every sentence in a piece of writing is not the same type, because that might make the writing dull or awkward for the reader. One way they do this is to mix simple, compound, and complex sentences in writing.

Read the simple sentences below. Then use the comma and the conjunction in parentheses to rewrite the two simple sentences as a compound sentence.

7. (and) Lightning rods are still in use today. They are especially handy in places like Florida, which have many storms.

8. (but) Many people think lightning is just a dangerous phenomena. Lightning returns negative energy to the earth, which produces nitrogen that plants need to grow.

0-7696-4057-5 *Proofreading and Editing*

Speak the Language

Sentences and Paragraphs

Editors check to make sure sentences are complete, but they also check to see if sentences are used in the best possible way. For instance, if an editor sees two short sentences that could be made into one sentence, he or she will do that, to make it more interesting for the reader. An editor may also take a compound sentence that is confusing because it is made of two clauses that do not belong together, and make it into two separate sentences.

Simple Sentence: Language is an important part of life.

Compound sentence: Language is an important part of life, because it fulfills our basic human need to communicate with one another.

Read the sentences below. Write S for simple sentence or C for compound sentence.

1. _____ There are between 5,000 and 10,000 languages spoken in the world.

2. _____ Some languages are spoken by very few people, and some are spoken by many.

3. _____ For instance, there is one African language that is spoken by only one person, but over one million people speak Chinese.

4. _____ Many think it's important to study another language, because only 200 people in Latvia speak a language called *Liv*.

5. _____ English is the most widespread language in the world.

6. _____ Over 470 million people speak English.

7. _____ Spanish is the second most-spoken language in the United States.

8. _____ What would you do if you were the last one to speak your language?

Speak the Language (cont.)

9. Which sentence on page 37 should be made into two sentences, because the sentences it is made of are not related to each other?

    a. sentence 8

    b. sentence 1

    c. sentence 4

10. Which two sentences on page 37 could be made into one sentence because they are related to the same topic?

    a. sentences 1 and 2

    b. sentences 5 and 6

    c. sentences 7 and 8

Read the following sentences. Join together simple sentences that should be joined into compound sentences. Separate compound sentences that should be separated. Use proofreading symbols.

I speak English. I also know a little French. I am going to learn Spanish. I think that knowing more than one language is important because I have met many people who are interested in learning a second language. If you know more than one language it can open doors for you in your career and many people enjoy learning a second language very much. You can learn a second language in school. You can also pick it up from living in a foreign country. Regardless of how you learn a second language you should consider doing it since many people all over the world know a second language and I think the world will be a better place if more people can communicate with one another.

London in 1601

Editors make sure sentences are complete. A sentence must have a subject, have a predicate (the part of the sentence that says something about the subject), and tell a complete thought. A **sentence fragment** is not a complete sentence because it does not have all the necessary parts. Read the following examples of complete sentences and sentence fragments.

Sentence: On the south is a bridge of stone eight hundred feet in length.

Sentence fragments: Paulus Jovius, in his description of the most remarkable towns in England.

The following sentences are from a description of the city of London written by an observer in the year 1601. Write an S on the line for sentences. Write F on the line before each fragment.

1. _____ The wealth of the world is wafted to it by the Thames.

2. _____ Navigable to merchant ships through a safe and deep channel for sixty miles.

3. _____ Its banks are everywhere beautified with fine country seats, woods, and farms.

4. _____ Below is the royal palace of Greenwich; above, that of London; and between both, on the west of London.

5. _____ Most remarkable for the courts of justice.

6. _____ This river abounds in swans, swimming in flocks.

7. _____ And St. Peter's Church, enriched with the royal tombs.

8. _____ The sight of them, and their noise, is vastly agreeable to the fleets that meet them in their course.

Sentences and Paragraphs:

Topic Sentences

Jessica's Activities

The main idea of a paragraph is called the topic. The sentence that expresses the topic is called the **topic sentence**. It is often the first sentence in the paragraph. An editor must make sure the topic sentence tells the main idea clearly.

Read the paragraph. Then answer the questions.

   Jessica got good grades on most of her schoolwork. She also excelled in several sports. She participated in intramurals for tennis, basketball, and golf, and often won. She was interested in drama, and acted in many of the school plays, though she did not always get the lead. In addition, she volunteered with her youth group for two local charities, and enjoyed doing that, too.

Circle the right answer.

1. The topic sentence is missing. What is the main idea of the passage?
    a. Jessica was too busy to take care of her school work.
    b. Jessica was much better at sports than she was at drama.
    c. Jessica was able to do a lot of different things.

2. Which of the following sentences would be the best topic sentence?
    a. Jessica managed to keep up a varied schedule of activities.
    b. Here is a list of Jessica's activities for you to read.
    c. Jessica was always worried about getting everything done.

3. Choose two details that could be added to the paragraph.
    a. Jessica did not like to work in group activities.
    b. Good time management was the key to Jessica's success.
    c. She found that sports gave her energy to work on her homework afterward.
    d. Her friend Jena didn't like to do any of these activities except tennis.

Doctor Anna

The sentence that expresses the main idea of a paragraph is called the **topic sentence**. The other sentences in the paragraph should all support the topic sentence. These sentences are called **supporting details** because they tell the reader more about the main idea. Every paragraph should have at least three supporting detail sentences for each topic sentence.

Circle the sentence that does not support the main idea.

1. When Doctor Anna returned home in 1828, she soon faced an epidemic that was sweeping through southern Illinois.

   a. Both people and animals were victims of a mysterious illness called "milk sickness."

   b. The wilderness of Illinois had few doctors.

   c. Anna lost her mother and sister-in-law to milk sickness.

2. She was determined to find the true cause of the disease.

   a. She wondered if something that the cattle ate caused the illness.

   b. She also noted that people might be contracting the illness from drinking tainted milk.

   c. Many settlers blamed witches for the illness.

3. Anna began doing fieldwork in the truest sense of the word: she headed to the fields and observed grazing cattle.

   a. Although horses, goats, and pigs were sometimes affected, cattle were the most frequent animal victims.

   b. One day when she was in the field following a heard, a Shawnee woman showed Dr. Anna a plant called white snakeroot.

   c. The Native American woman suggested this poisonous plant might be causing the problem.

4. Doctor Anna set up an experiment to test the Shawnee woman's theory about the white snakeroot.

   a. After feeding white snakeroot to a calf, she was able to prove that the plant caused milk sickness.

   b. Her notes revealed that milk sickness became serious in the summer, and then abated after the first frost in the autumn.

   c. Anna began a campaign to convince farmers in the area to get rid of these plants.

Sentences and Paragraphs

Canoes

A **paragraph** is a group of sentences that tells the reader about one idea. This is a paragraph:

The topic sentence tells the main idea of the paragraph. Often, the topic sentence comes first. The rest of the sentences tell more about the main idea. These are called supporting sentences. For a paragraph to make sense, all the sentences in it must be about that one main idea. The reader can tell a new paragraph has begun, because the first line of the paragraph is indented, which means the first word is moved in from the left side.

Remember that paragraphs have a formula:

● The first line is indented.

● The first sentence is usually the topic sentence.

● The other sentences support the topic sentence with details.

Read each paragraph. Then choose the number of the sentence that does not belong in the paragraph.

1. (1) Canoes have been around for hundreds of years and have been made in all shapes and sizes. (2) Generally, a canoe is thought of as a boat that is pointed at both ends with a relatively flat bottom. (3) It is wider in the middle than at the ends. (4) I've been on many canoeing trips with my family. (5) Canoes are usually propelled by paddles, but some can also be sailed.

   a. sentence 2   c. sentence 4

   b. sentence 3   d. sentence 5

2. (1) A kayak is a form of a canoe. (2) The kayak was developed by the Inuit natives of Greenland, the Arctic Circle, and the Hudson Bay coasts of North America. (3) These natives made kayaks by constructing frames of driftwood or animal bones, which they bound together with gut. (4) The frame was covered completely in sealskin, except for a hole at the top that created the cockpit. (5) A kayak is fun to use when on vacation at the lake. (6) The sealskin, which was sewn onto the frame, was naturally waterproof.

   a. sentence 5

   b. sentence 1

   c. sentence 6

   d. sentence 3

0-7696-4057-5 *Proofreading and Editing*

When the Chips Are Down

Sentences and Paragraphs

A paragraph is a group of sentences that tells the reader about one particular main idea. If sentences do not support the main idea, they do not belong in the paragraph. The editor must know when a new paragraph starts.

Each paragraph should have a clear topic sentence. The sentences in each paragraph should support the topic sentences.

Read the following report below and on page 44. Use proofreading marks to fix the mistakes. Show where new paragraphs should begin. Insert quotation marks where they are missing. Remember that when a new person speaks in a story, a new paragraph should begin.

This just won't work, Dexter, Sean said. The pins are too loose on the chip. Maybe we can repair it. We sure can't afford a new chip like that one, replied Sean's friend, Dexter. Then Dexter dropped by. Dexter's garage felt cooler than the sultry weather outside. It was too hot to work. Still, there was only a week and a half before the science fair. What would they do when the fair was over? Sean tried to reconnect the pin to the computer chip. Oh, no! It broke again, Dex. This just isn't going to work, growled Sean. What do you think we should do now? questioned Dexter. Sean simply shook his head. He knew that there was too little time to get enough money to buy the computer chip they needed to control the robot's "brain."

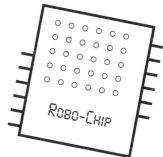

ROBO-CHIP

Sentences and Paragraphs

When the Chips Are Down

Mom, would you be willing to lend me some money? We need it to finish our robot for the science fair, Dexter said to his mother as she fixed dinner. You know I would help if I could, Honey, but we just don't have the money right now. his mother answered. His mother asked Dexter why he needed the money. The boys became determined to earn money any way they could. Dexter washed cars for some people up the block. Sean cleaned at his father's shop after the workers left at night. They had only two days to go until the science fair. Dexter and Sean slowly counted the money. They had only two days to go until the science fair. Dexter and Sean slowly counted the money. They had $62.30. They were $18.70 short. It was time to tell their science teacher, Mrs. Frommer. We tried, Mrs. Frommer, but we just couldn't make enough money for the chip for our robot's brain, the students told her sadly. Mrs. Frommer smiled. I have just the thing! she said. She opened her desk drawer and took out a slip of paper. it was a 25% off coupon for the local computer store. When Sean and Dexter stood proudly next to their science fair exhibit, they had a robot that came to life.

Name _____   Date _____

High Tech Tale

One of an editor's jobs is to make sure that all the sentences in a piece of writinge are in the correct order. If a story or report presents ideas in an order that does not make sense to the reader, it will be confusing and ineffective.

Read the sentences below from a story about using computers. Below are several sentences lettered, but they are not in the correct order. Put a number from 1 to 10 next to each sentence, to show the order you believe the sentences go in to make the most sense.

_____ a.   It was the summer of 2020. I was 15 years old, and a computer changed my life.

_____ b.   When Jeremy and I took the high-speed train downtown to the library, we missed our stop and ended up two cities away.

_____ c.   After a week, my parents burst into my room with an Internet officer, who unplugged my computer right in the middle of a game. I howled with rage as I was taken off to the Center for Online Addiction, but I needed help.

_____ d.   By the end of the summer, I was much better, but was forbidden any computer use for six months. Instead, I was given an ancient machine called a "typewriter" to use for reports and papers.

_____ e.   The characters in the game became more real to me than my own friends. In fact, I began refusing calls and emails from my friends, and I never went to family meals.

_____ f.   I realized the computer was a magic carpet, a door into any world I wanted to explore.

_____ g.   Around a dark corner under the elevated train tracks, we saw a dingy storefront. It featured a virtual-reality smorgasbord of computer gear and video games.

_____ h.   I had lost 20 pounds and was suffering from both malnutrition and sleep deprivation.

_____ i.   Within days, I was addicted to my new game. It was a virtual-reality fantasy.

_____ j.   I was put in the hospital wing of the center. Meanwhile, my mother and father packed up my computer and sent it to an elementary school.

Sentences and Paragraphs:

Reported Speech

At Sheila's House

Paragraphs are made of sentences that all support the main idea. When you begin to write about a new idea, you need to start a new paragraph. Another reason to start a new paragraph has to do with **reported speech,** which is telling what someone said, in a story. In a story, whenever a different character speaks, the writer begins a new paragraph. The editor must make sure this is done properly.

Use the ¶ mark to show where new paragraphs start in this story.

No one was home when they got to Sheila's house. No one ever seemed to be home at Sheila's house. Kelly had two sisters and a brother. "It must be amazing to have the whole house to yourself. I'm lucky if I can be alone for five minutes," said Kelly. "It's awesome," Sheila replied. "I can do whatever I want. Do you want to order a pizza? There's nothing in the refrigerator." There was never anything in Sheila's refrigerator. "That's okay," said Kelly. "I have to go home for dinner soon." Sheila rolled her eyes. "I would go crazy if people were telling me what to do all the time." "Well, you're lucky," said Kelly. Sheila was lucky. She had perfect hair, perfect clothes, a perfect house. "I would give anything to be Sheila for just one day," thought Kelly. The phone rang. "Hi, Mom," Kelly heard Sheila say. "No, it's okay. I understand." She hung up. "My mom's having dinner out again," she said. "Are you sure you can't stay for pizza?" "Sorry. I have to go or I'll be late for dinner," said Kelly. "Whatever. See you." Kelly saw Sheila looking out the window as she walked down the street. Suddenly, Sheila's house looked very big, and Sheila looked very small.

Name _____   Date _____

Mathew Brady's Career

Sentences and Paragraphs

A paragraph is a group of sentences that tells the reader about one idea. Editors must know where paragraphs end and where they begin. They also need to check that paragraphs are written in an order that makes sense.

Read the following report about Mathew Brady. In the blanks, number the paragraphs to show their correct order.

_____ a. Mathew Brady tried to end warfare for all time. He used a new, powerful weapon. He used a camera.

_____ b. Brady did not stop warfare with his work, but he did raise the awareness of the costs of war among common citizens. After the Civil War, people lost interest in his chronicle of the war. Because he could find few buyers for his photographs and did not earn enough money to pay for his wartime work, Brady went bankrupt.

_____ c. Brady believed that photography could serve an important purpose. His images could create a record of national life. When the Civil War broke out, he wanted to document the war as a part of that record. Brady started to take photographs of war scenes. He assembled a corps of photographers who worked in the field, taking photographs of battle scenes and military life. His efforts culminated in an 1862 display of photographs made after the Battle of Antietam. The bloodshed shocked the visitors to the exhibit, most of whom had never scene a field of battle.

_____ d. Brady opened his first photography studio in 1844. The images he produced were *daguerreotypes*, not the photographs he would take later. Daguerreotypes recorded images on sheets of copper coated with silver. They required long exposures, so the person being photographed would have to stay perfectly still for three to 15 minutes. By 1855, Brady was advertising a new type of image that had just been invented: a photograph made on paper.

_____ e. Years after the war, Congress bought Brady's collection. It is now considered a priceless documentation of the War between the States. Other photographs by Mathew Brady sell for thousands of dollars and are considered national treasures.

Published by Milestone. Copyright protected.

0-7696-4057-5 *Proofreading and Editing*

Name _____ Date _____

Tell All about It

The reader must be able to understand the reason, or purpose, a writer wrote something. The editor must check to make sure that this purpose is clear to see. He or she must also know who the readers, or audience, will be. The title of a piece of writing can tell the reader a lot about the purpose of a piece of writing and its intended audience.

Circle the letter of the best title for each audience and purpose.

1. Audience: your parents

    Purpose: a story about an exciting event at school

    a. The Homecoming Parade

    b. Statistics on School Performance

    c. Just Another Day

2. Audience: your friends from school

    Purpose: a report on the fun of rock climbing

    a. A Rockin' Sport

    b. Rock Climbing: an Activity for All Ages

    c. The Dangers of Rock Climbing

3. Audience: the school staff

    Purpose: tell about the upcoming school awards ceremony

    a. Who Will Win It?

    b. Our Annual Academic Awards

    c. Past School Awards Winners: Where Are They Now?

4. Audience: the Math Club

    Purpose: to tell about new math competition strategies

    a. Fun with Numbers

    b. Basic Math Formulas

    c. New Ways to Win the Math Battle

Write titles for the following audience and purpose.

5. Audience: your class

    Purpose: to tell about your vacation

    _____

6. Audience: the readers of the school newspaper

    Purpose: a debate about school issues.

    _____

Name _____ Date _____

Pick a Purpose

There are several different purposes of writing: to inform, to entertain, or to persuade.

Read the audience and purpose. Choose the best topic to match.

1. Audience: classmates and teacher

   Purpose: to tell about your family's background

   a. your grandfather's immigration from France

   b. your family trip to the beach

   c. your interest in the subject of genealogy

2. Audience: your friends

   Purpose: to tell a funny story about a pet

   a. how your kitten steals tuna off your plate

   b. the judging rules at a dog show

   c. the need to make sure all dogs and cats are immunized

3. Audience: student driver

   Purpose: to inform of important safety rules

   a. why it takes time to get a driver's license

   b. the best way to study for your learner's permit test

   c. why you should not use the cell phone while driving

4. Audience: school building committee

   Purpose: to persuade committee to accept new building plans

   a. the school doesn't need any more work

   b. workers don't want to build anything for the school

   c. why a gymnasium would be the best addition to the school

5. Audience: your best friend

   Purpose: to tell him or her about something that is important to you

   a. how long it usually takes to do your homework

   b. taking homework seriously as part of your education

   c. why he should do your homework for you

Name _____ Date _____

A Famous Composer

Titles and **subtitles** make reports and articles easier to read. A title can give a reader an idea of what a report or article will be about, before he or she reads it. It can both tell something about the main idea of the report or article, and get the reader excited about reading it. In a similar way, a subtitle can tell the reader what a section of the report or article will be about, and make it seem interesting to the reader. An editor looks to see if titles and subtitles are written in such a way, that they do their jobs properly. (Hint: titles and subtitles should have each word capitalized, except for articles and prepositions, like *the* or *of*.)

Read the following report about a famous composer. Then answer the questions on page 51 about good titles and subtitles.

(1) Can you imagine a five-year-old composing music and then playing it on a child-sized violin? This was a part of the childhood of Wolfgang Amadeus Mozart, a young genius who grew up to be one of the most creative composers of all time. He was born in Salzburg, Austria, in January of 1756.

(2) Wolfgang Amadeus Mozart was remarkable. He could listen to any piece of music once and then play it from memory. He could play the keyboard or the violin blindfolded. Music that Mozart wrote at the age of five was as good as works by many adult composers of the time.

(3) As an adult, Mozart earned his living by selling his compositions, giving concerts, and providing music lessons to the wealthy. None of these ventures earned him much money, and he spent far more than he was able to earn.

(4) When Mozart was a young man, he fell in love with a German singer, a woman named Alyosia Weber. He wanted to give up his career to help hers, but his parents forbade it. Mozart postponed his wedding plans, and when he tried to return to the relationship, Alyosia rejected him. Instead, Mozart married her younger sister, Constanze Weber. The young couple never had much money, but they were devoted to each other. They loved to attend parties and balls.

(5) To earn money, Mozart wrote operas. Some of his most famous works were *The Marriage of Figaro*, *The Magic Flute*, and *Don Giovanni*, all of which are still performed today. Mozart also wrote music for the court of the Emperor of Austria. Mozart often waited until the last moment to work on pieces that had been commissioned, or paid for in advance. For example, he did not write the overture to Don Giovanni until the night before it was going to be performed!

(6) By the spring of 1791, Mozart was ill and depressed. He was deeply in debt. His health, which had never been good, was declining. He was visited by a stranger who asked Mozart to write a requiem, a musical work for a funeral. Mozart agreed to take the commission, but then he began to fear that the requiem was actually being written for his own death. Unfortunately, his fears were justified. Mozart died in December of 1791, at the age of 35.

A Famous Composer (cont.)

Editing:

Titles and Subtitles

1. Which would be the best title for this article?
   a. The Amazing Amadeus
   b. Mozart's Opera Works
   c. Great Composers of the 1700's

2. Which of the following would be the best subtitle for paragraph number 1?
   a. Where Did Amadeus Come From?
   b. A Child Genius
   c. A Future Composer

3. Which of the following would be the best subtitle for paragraph number 2?
   a. The Great Touring Mozarts
   b. A Talented Young Musician
   c. A Competitor at Five

4. Which of the following would be the best subtitle for paragraph number 3?
   a. Meeting Wealthy Friends
   b. Trying to Make Ends Meet with Music
   c. A Variety of Musical Projects

5. Which of the following would be the best subtitle for paragraph number 4?
   a. Eternal Love for Aloysia
   b. A Postponed Wedding
   c. Marriage to Constanze

6. Which of the following words should definitely be included in paragraph number 5?
   a. Emperor
   b. Operas
   c. Don Giovanni

7. Which of the following subtitles might make the reader the most interested in reading further?
   a. Mozart Dies
   b. Health Problems
   c. A Mysterious Coincidence

Editing:

Paraphrase

Simplicity

Paraphrasing is a way of expressing the same idea, in different ways, using different words. An editor checks to see if there is a better way to express ideas in a piece of writing.

One way to express an idea might be:

It appeared to be completely uneccessarary for us to carry any type of protective rain device, as there was no trace of humidity in the atmosphere.

A simpler way to paraphrase might be:

We didn't think we needed to bring an umbrella, since it didn't look like it was going to rain.

Sometimes an editor will suggest a more vibrant way of writing something.

One way to express an idea might be:

He was tired. It made him fall asleep fast.

Could be paraphrased as:

He was so utterly exhausted that he collapsed into bed and quickly fell into slumber.

Read the following sentences. In the lines below, follow the suggestions to write a good paraphrase of each one.

1. My math homework is hard. I'm having trouble with it. (more complex)

   _____

2. We drove swiftly to the seaside in order to facilitate an early start for a lovely day at the shore. (more simple)

   _____

3. The flower smells good. (use prettier language)

   _____

4. My friend Jeff, who is also a friend of my friend Alan, wanted to come over to work on a project that is being worked on by all three of us for the science class that we are all in. (make less complicated and confusing)

   _____

Simplicity (cont.)

Editing:

Paraphrase

Sometimes a writer paraphrases information for an article or report that he or she found in another source. The editor must read that source, and check to see that the writer paraphrased the information correctly.

Read each part of the report about George Washington Carver. Choose the sentence that best paraphrases the paragraph.

5. George Washington Carver was born in Missouri in 1864. He was born a slave. As a child he became interested in plants. People even called him "the plant doctor." When he was 12, he went away to school. He got a job to pay his way and lived with families who would take him in. By 1896, he had earned two college degrees. He became a teacher at the Tuskegee Institute in Alabama.

   a. The author tells how George Washington Carver was born in slavery in Missouri. From the time Carver was young child, he was very interested in plants. At 12, he went to school and worked to pay for his schooling. He earned two college degrees and became a teacher at the Tuskegee Institute.

   b. The author tells about George Washington Carver as a child. Carver was born in 1864. People called him "the plant doctor." When he was 12, he started school. Eventually, he earned two college degrees. Then he got a job to pay back the money for his schooling.

6. Carver is best known for his work in agriculture. To help farmers, he experimented to develop new products made from peanuts and sweet potatoes, plants that would enrich the soil. From peanuts, he made more than 300 new products, including coffee, cheese, milk, ink, flour, and soap. He also made more than 100 new products from sweet potatoes, including molasses, flour, rubber, and glue. For his work, Carver received many honors. He was proud of the work he did to help farmers.

   a. The author tells about Carver's experiments with plants. Carver invented many products, such as ink and soap. He also discovered how to make molasses. For these inventions, Carver received many honors.

   b. The author tells how Carver decided to help farmers by finding new ways to make products from peanuts and sweet potatoes. He experimented with the plants. He discovered more than 300 new ways to use peanuts and more than 100 ways to use sweet potatoes. He was awarded many honors because of his work.

Editing:

Problem Words

Dinner in a Restaurant

Some words are confusing to use correctly. There are sets of words which sound alike, but are spelled differently and have different meanings. These sets of words are called **homophones**. An editor must make sure the writer has used the correct word in a set of homophones.

A teacher usually takes *roll* at the beginning of a class.

An actor plays a *role* in a movie.

A small round ball of bread is also called a *roll*.

Proofread the following story about dinner in a restaurant. Make sure the proper homophones have been used. To delete a word use the ⌐ mark. To insert a new word use the ∧ mark.

As we road to the restaurant, I realized I was getting vary hungry. The restaurant was modern in design, decorated outside in stainless steal. I wasn't sure what to where before we had left home, but when we got their, I could see I was perfectly dressed.

My mom is a vegetarian, so she wanted to order something without any meet. But I had my heart set on having a big, juicy stake!

"Deer," said my mom, "Wood you please pass the salt?"

"Write away, Mom," I said, as I handed it to her.

Both of hour dinners were delicious. The salad dressing was maid just the way I like it. After we had dinner, Mom asked if I wanted desert.

"I definitely due!" I said. There most popular desert was cheesecake. Fortunately, they're was one peace left. My mom got something suite to, even though she's trying to loose wait.

Check the Source

Another proofreading job for editors, is to check to see that writers have correctly used information from sources. Sources are different places the writer got from information from when doing research. A writer must use sources that are reliable and correct. Sources may include newspapers, interviews, books, articles, and online Web sites. An editor makes sure that facts, dates, and other pieces of information are correct.

Choose which source or sources would help you the most to proofread and check each piece of writing.

1. A newspaper article about your school board's election
   a. interview with a school board member
   b. article about school district student testing
   c. a blueprint of the school's building

2. A project on 18th century furniture
   a. the encyclopedia
   b. a book on 18th century explorers
   c. a newspaper article about new furniture styles

3. A book report on Charlotte's Web
   a. an article on spiders
   b. a book about the author
   c. a copy of the book

4. Instructions on how to bake banana bread
   a. a book on importation of bananas
   b. a cooking book
   c. an article on the history of the banana bread recipe

5. What sources could you use to help you check a story about the history of the space program?

   _____

   _____

Name _____ Date _____

An editor makes sure that facts, dates, and other details in the piece of writing are right. The sources help the editor do this. Sometimes the editor must check information from two sources. The sources may have different information.

Samir is writing a report about Benjamin Franklin. He took notes from two sources, a timeline he found in an encyclopedia and an article on a Web site about American history he found on the Internet. Read Samir's notes. Then check his writing to see if he has gotten any of the information wrong.

Source 1: Timeline

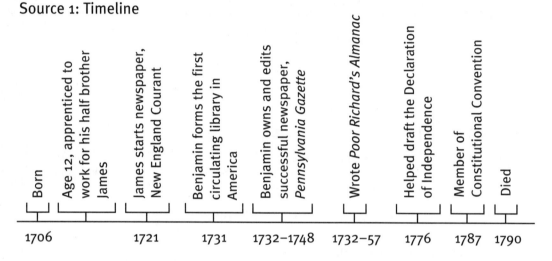

Source 2: Benjamin Franklin (from Web site on Internet)

   I.   Was a versatile man of many talents: printer, publisher, author, inventor, scientist, philosopher, statesman, and diplomat.

  II.   In 1727, he formed the Junto Club, a discussion group for self-improvement, which in 1743 developed into the American Philosophical Society

 III.   From 1753 to 1754, Franklin served as postmaster general of the Colonies.

  IV.   Franklin was sent to England and France on diplomatic issues many times, and altogether, he lived 25 years abroad, in London and Paris. This gave him an international view of the world in a time when most people only thought about local issues.

   V.   He was released from his diplomatic duties in 1785; he returned home.

  VI.   His last job for his country was as a member of the Constitutional Congress, where his talents for bringing people together in compromise helped bring our constitution into existence.

Benjamin Franklin (cont.)

Editing:

Sources

Samir's Report:

Benjamin Franklin was a man of many talents who had an incredible life. Born in 1712, he was first introduced to the newspaper publishing world by his brother James. Benjamin became an apprentice, and helped his brother on James' newspaper, the *Pennsylvania Gazette*. From 1732 to 1748, Benjamin wrote and published his *Poor Richards Almanac*.

Franklin served the colonial government in many ways. From 1753 to 1754, he was a member of the Constitutional Congress. He lived in England and France for many years, performing diplomatic duties. In 1785, he retired from public life, and privately worked on his inventions and writing. He died in 1790, having had an amazing life of accomplishments.

1. What information could Samir have included from the sources to make the report more complete?

    a. Franklin's personal life

    b. More about Franklin as an inventor

    c. Franklin's taste in clothing

    d. both a and b

2. Samir made several mistakes in this report. Check all the facts against the sources and underline the mistakes.

3. Where could Samir have found information about Franklin's inventions?

    _____

4. What source did Samir use to find out about Franklin's diplomatic work?

    _____

0-7696-4057-5 *Proofreading and Editing*

Editing Different Genres:

Checklists

Checking the List

Using a checklist makes editing and proofreading easier. As the editor looks at the writing, he or she is reminded of all the types of mistakes to look for, by keeping the checklist nearby. Since there are many different types of writing, the items on an editing checklist should match whatever is being edited. Some mistakes, like spelling errors, should be included on every checklist. Other mistakes are only found in some specific types of writing.

Read each question. Circle all that apply.

1. Which items would you edit for every type of writing?
   - a. spelling
   - b. punctuation
   - c. appropriate word choice
   - d. comma after greeting
   - e. quotations
   - f. misplaced modifiers
   - g. correct date and greeting
   - h. fits audience and purpose
   - i. beginning, middle, and end

2. Which two items would you not need to edit for a letter?
   - a. clear and complete explanation
   - b. commas after the greeting and closing
   - c. comma between date and year
   - d. good conclusion

3. Which items would you need to edit for instructions?
   - a. clear and complete steps
   - b. correct use of quotation marks
   - c. fits audience and purpose
   - d. use of titles and subtitles

4. Which items would you need to check when editing a story?
   - a. quotations
   - b. fits audience and purpose
   - c. supporting details
   - d. correct information from sources

5. Which items would you check when reading a report?
   - a. fits audience and purpose
   - b. appropriate word choice
   - c. subject-verb agreement
   - d. punctuation

Checking the List (cont.)

Read the following piece of writing. Use the checklist to edit. Use proofreading marks to fix the mistakes.

Checklist

- ☐ spelling
- ☐ capitalization
- ☐ punctuation
- ☐ topic sentence and supporting details used correctly

wher can you find 100 million year old dinasore blood. From amber a substance known more for it's decorative uses than for its scientifec value. That is. until recently.

Amber is actually hardened tree resin that has been fossilized? perhaps the height of ambers decorative powers could be seen in a russian Palace. Most of it is mined in the baltic sea area. It is smooth and warms quickly to the touch. the ancshent greeks called it electron, perhaps because amber builds up a small, negative charge when it is rubbed.

in the 1700s, an entire room of 100,000 carved amber pieces were given as a gift to Tsar peter the Great of Russia. This Golden room lit by more than 500 candles was said to be dazzling in its beautry.

0-7696-4057-5 *Proofreading and Editing*

Editing Different Genres:

Letters

Editing Letters

The checklist you might use to proofread and edit a letter needs to remind you about specific details. For instance, there should be a comma between the day of the month and the year. A comma should also follow a greeting and a closing. The **tone** or attitude of a friendly letter should be just that: friendly and informal. A business letter needs a different tone and more formal language. Otherwise, you might upset or offend the reader. Think for a second: would you speak to your teacher the same way you speak to your little brother?

Read the following letters. The first one is a letter from one friend to another. The second letter is a business letter. Proofread both letters, using the following checklist to remind you about things you need to look for:

☐ spelling	☐ indentation
☐ capitalization	☐ grammar
☐ punctuation	☐ type of greeting and closing
☐ comma between date and year	☐ overall tone
☐ comma after greeting and closing	

A Friendly Letter

july10 2005

Dear Jamal

well Summer vacation is more than haff over but i whish it would never end. Besides going to the town pool alot, me and my brother hav got to see three good movies so far? Wer'e lucky because the local theatar has haff prize admission on Wednesday afternoons. We were able to make some money mowing launs for a few of hour neighbors. I would like to sincerely express my best wishes to you for continued financial success in your own entrepenurial efforts with your lemonade stand.

You would of lovd one of the movies we saw, called Dont run its right behind you. Its a comedy that makes fun of horror movies.

I'll see you in September!

Your friend,

Shannon

1. What does not need to be edited in the letter on page 61?
    a. indentation
    b. capitals in the title
    c. punctuation
    d. clear steps

A Business Letter

May 8, 2005

Dear Mr. Malcolm,

    This letter is in regard to our meeting, scheduled for thursday the 20 of May. i recently get a phon messege from your asistant, who told me that you would have to postpone the meating. What's up with that?

    Unfortunately its not conveinent for me to re-schedule any meetings at all for the next month. I hav not be able to reech ether you or your assistant on the phone for several days.

Would you pleas ask her to call me soon, in order to determine another time for our meeting. thankyou for your assistance in this matter.

Sincerely,

Ms. Farley

2. What did not need to be changed in this letter?
    a. spelling
    b. commas after greeting and date
    c. correct directions
    d. capitalization

Name _____ Date _____

The purpose of a report is to give information. Therefore, it is very important that the information in a report be clear and correct. The facts in the report must match the facts in the source, the place where the writer found the information.

Read the following report and notes from sources. Then answer the questions on page 63.

Life in Yakutia

Many people who live in colder climates look forward to spring? So imagine. a place that is so cold that a temperature just above freezing is considered a warm day.

A place like this exists in a region of russia called Yakutia. Located in the Eastern part of Russia known as Siberia, it is one of the coldest areas in the world. In the town of yakutsk, inhabitants have stated that it gets so cold that a corridor forms in the shape of a silhouette when a person walks down the street. The person's body heat actually cuts a path through the icy air a path that others can see. After a person has past out of sight, the corridor remains, hanging in the bright, cold air. Some parts of Siberia receive between 30 and 50 inches (76–127 cm) of snow each year. But Yakutia has very little precipitation. You mite think this is a good thing, but as a result, the region lacks the natural insulation that snow provides. The Yakutians layer the snow that does fall over their houses to form icy coatings to retain the heat. A traditional yakutian house is a two-story, round hut with a nearly flat roof. It is made completely of mud, which also acts as insulation against the bitter cold.

Permafrost is ground made up of ice and soil that stays frozen for most of the year. In fact, half of the land mass of the former Soviet Union rests on permafrost. Permafrost causes problems because it has an active layer that freezes in the winter and thaws during the summer. The thickness of this layer ranges from 8 to 10 feet (0.9–3 m). Everything in Yakutia is built on permafrost. With the ground shifting so dramatically, it makes the construction of roads, buildings, pipelines, and other structures difficult.

You might think that spring and summer would give the people of Yakutia a special sense of relief, but you would be wrong. When the temperatures rise, their houses sink as the permafrost gives way. Sometimes only the roofs of houses can be seen from the street. Temperatures above freezing mean chaos in Yakutia. Mud oozes everywhere and tiny rivers of melted snow flood towns and settlements. When winter returns, stability returns with it. Houses, roads, and the ground itself stay glued together like the pieces of a model-train village. Paths and roads become passable again. In winter, life returns to normal.

Name _____   Date _____

Life in Yakutia (cont.)

Source 1: Glossary

   precipitation: condensed moisture in the air

   insulation: something used as a separating layer, to keep heat or cold, in.

   permafrost: a layer of ice and soil on the ground that stays frozen most of the year.

Source 2: Notes from article about Yakutia in northern Russia

   I.   Residents are used to intense cold.

   II. Snow actually helps to keep houses warm, by acting as insulation

   III. Traditional house is a one-story, rectangular cabin, made with logs sealed with mud

   IV. Permafrost ranges in thickness from 3 to 10 feet

   IV. Warm weather creates problems for people; when ice melts, houses sink into mud

1. What is the main idea of this report?

   _____

2. Write two sentences that support the main idea.

   _____

3. Reread the report. Use the checklist below to edit the report.

☐ spelling	☐ topic sentences and supporting details
☐ capitalization	☐ indentation
☐ punctuation	☐ clear and correct details
☐ subject-verb agreement	☐ facts match the source material

4. What kind of picture could have been included to make this report easier to understand?

   _____

5. How could the author use Source 1?

   _____

Editing Different Genres:

Reports

Unscrambling Script

The purpose of a report is to give information. Therefore, it is very important that the information in a report be clear and correct. The facts in the report must match the facts in the source, the place where the writer found the information.

Read the report below, and then answer the questions that follow.

Although pictorial characters was used to represent comon objects by several ancient peoples, including the Greeks, Hittites, Cretans, and Mayans, Egyptian hieroglyphs are the most frequently studied pictograms. Egyptians communicated with hieroglyphs from about 3940 BC until about AD 300. Hieroglyphs continued to be used in som religious texts until the early forth century AD Egyptian hieroglyphs presented and unsolvd mystery to historians until the eighteenth century? they were sometimes written horizontally, and sometimes vertically, they seemed to be symbolic, but some argued that they could be interpreted phonetically. Then Napoleon's army discovered the Rosetta Stone in egypt in 1789. The stone, which states a decree from Ptolemy V in three different languages, enabld Egyptian born Jean François Champollion and others to interpret many different hieroglyphics from two different eras, by comparing them to each other, and to mayan words on the stone! He finds that some of the symbols pictorially represented objects, some symbols meant specific sounds, and some symbols used pictures of object to stand for homonyms of the pictured world. Egyptologists and Linguists have studied the fascinating ancient script to such a degree that little remains a mystery about hieroglyphics.

Source: Timeline of hieroglyphics

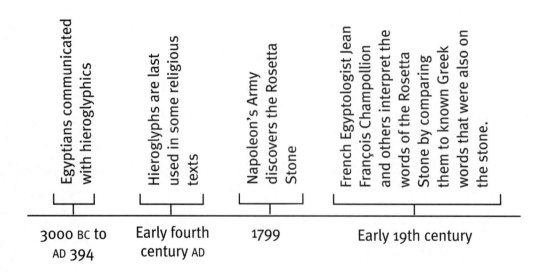

| Egyptians communicated with hieroglyphics | Hieroglyphs are last used in some religious texts | Napoleon's Army discovers the Rosetta Stone | French Egyptologist Jean François Champollion and others interpret the words of the Rosetta Stone by comparing them to known Greek words that were also on the stone. |
| 3000 BC to AD 394 | Early fourth century AD | 1799 | Early 19th century |

Unscrambling Script (cont.)

Editing Different Genres:

Reports

1. Why do you think the author wrote this report?

   a. to tell the reader about fun of learning a second language

   b. to tell the reader about the life of Ptolemy V of Egypt.

   c. to tell the reader about a fascinating historic discovery about language

2. Use the source provided to find the errors in this report. Underline them in the story and write the corrected sentences on the lines below.

   _____

   _____

   _____

   _____

3. Which vocabulary words could the writer have explained to make the report more understandable?

   a. phonetically

   b. symbols

   c. homonyms

   d. both a and c

4. Reread the report. Use the checklist below to edit the report.

   ☐ spelling

   ☐ capitalization

   ☐ punctuation

   ☐ subject-verb agreement

   ☐ indentation

   ☐ clear and correct details

   ☐ facts match the source material

Editing Different Genres:

Narratives

The Baseball Card

Another kind of writing an editor might have to work with is a **narrative**. A narrative is a tale or story that talks about either fictional or real events in the order they happened. Besides proofreading for the kinds of mistakes previously studied, an editor may check to make sure that the events described in the narrative make sense to the reader, and that they seem to be in the correct order.

Read the narrative below, and then answer the questions on page 67.

Wagner had played with the Pirates until the outbreak of World War I. Nearly 20 years later, he had been one of the first players inducted into the Baseball Hall of Fame. Mark looked at the old man and knew he did not realize what a treasure he had. I have to keep my hand from shaking, thought mark as he picked up the baseball card. The air in the swap meet seemed too suddenly warm. He stared at the early twentieth-century image and then slowly turned the card over. "That's one of my favorites," said the elderly man. "My dad got that in a pack of gum when he was a boy." "How...how much?" asked Mark. He cleared his voice. The man thought for a minute. "Fifty dollars," he said. Then he bit his lip. Maybe it was to much to ask, especially from a bog. Mark felt his hed swiming. The baseball card was in perfect condition. It showed the open, friendly face of Honus Wagner, a player from the Pittsburgh Pirates. The man watched Mark as he studied the card. I sure could use that $50, the man thought. He would settle for $40, but he wanted to see what the boy would say first. Mark looked at the man's face and the fraid collar of his shirt. I've never seen him at one of these swap meets before, thought Mark. I bet he is here because he needs some money, not because he knows a lot about baseball cards. Mark closed his eyes for a moment. What do I do? he asked himself. If I made this trade, it would be the biggest thing that ever happened to me. But I would have to remember that I robbed this man for the rest of my life. The man looked at the boy hopefully, and then his heart sank as Mark shook his head and handed back the card. How will I pay for that prescription? he wondered. Mark hesitated for a minute, and then he leaned forward.

The Baseball Card (cont.)

Editing Different Genres:

Narratives

1. Use the following checklist to edit the story.

☐ spelling

☐ punctuation

☐ capitalization

☐ story elements (beginning, middle, end)

☐ indentation

2. From whose point of view is the story told?

_____

3. What question has not been answered at the end of the story?

_____

_____

4. Show how you would answer the question by writing an ending to the story.

_____

_____

_____

_____

_____

_____

_____

_____

_____

_____

0-7696-4057-5 *Proofreading and Editing*

Name _____ Date _____

Read the narrative below, written in the voice of a sailor on one of Columbus' ships. Then answer the questions that follow.

Our voyage is begun. I wish now that I have not signed on to this ship for this dreadful journey. All seems well when we were loding our supplies and making the usual preparations. But now, a month later, I fear a curse has fallen over this ship. Only three day after we left, our mast has damage. The *Santa María* and the *Niña* helped us get to port for repairs. the *Pinta* was seaworthy again after a few weeks. Now, we sailed into the west day after day. The men whisper among themselves. They told tales of terrible monsters who are waiting to devour our ship when we arrive at the edge of the ocean.

Our situation worses, but there may be a small hope of saving ourselves. For days now, the crew have grown more and more vocal about how long we have sailed without seeing anything but water, streching in all directions. Finally, some of the older sailors went to captain Pinzón with their fears. He speaked directly to the Lord Admiral himself. Afterward, our three ships changed direction to the Southwest. I pray that this shift in direction will keep us from sailing off the edge of the world a rumor has it that we will try this heading for a few days only, and then turn back. I may never go to sea again, should I be fortunat enuf to find my way safly home.

A miracle has ocurred. Señor cerdá saw a large piece of driftwood yesterday afternoon. Amid great excitement, Captain Pinzón examined it. he said that since the wood was not smooth, it could not have been in the watter for long. Then early this morning the lookout on the *Santa María* spotted some birds. The crew did their work feverishly, scanning the horizon at every other moment. Finally, we heard our own lookout's cry, the one we had waited for every day. "Land? Land?" There it were, green and hazy on the horizon under a bank of low clouds. Not monsters, but land! I am fearful of these savage sea creatures, an just as fearful of the never-ending sea and the man who seem to beleve we can find land where no land exists.

Geraldo's Journal (cont.)

1. What can you tell about the narrator of this story?

   _____

   _____

2. What extra information might have made the narrative character more real?

   a. a discussion of the food served on the ship

   b. a tale of why the character went to sea

   c. an explanation of why sailors once believed in sea monsters

3. What is Geraldo's main fear in the story?

   _____

   _____

4. Is his fear resolved? What happens?

   _____

   _____

5. What information might have been included in the story to allow the reader to understand the historical content better?

   a. dates for all his journal entries

   b. the name of the ship Geraldo was on

   c. the number of men on Geraldo's ship

   d. all of the above

6. Use the following checklist to edit the story. Mark all mistakes with proofreading marks.

☐ spelling	☐ subject-verb agreement
☐ capitalization	☐ story elements (beginning, middle, end)
☐ punctuation	☐ indentation

Name _____ Date _____

The Bee Is Not Afraid of Me

Poetry discusses feelings, ideas, or events. Editing poetry is different than editing other forms of writing because there are certain things you don't need to think about when editing poetry. For instance, there is no topic sentence in a poem, so you don't have to look out for that. However, you must remember that the first word of every line in a poem must be capitalized. Every word in a poem is very important to its meaning, so an editor must make very sure that the writer has used the correct form of a word to express the intended idea.

Read the following poem, which needs editing.

The bee Is Not Afraid of Me

The bee is not afrayde of me,

i know the butterfly

The prety people in the woods

Receive me cordialy.

The brooks laughs louder when I com,

The breezes madder play?

Wherefore, mine eyes, thy sylver mists?

Wherefore, O summer's day?

by Emily Dickinson

1. Which checklist is best for editing this poem?

   a.
   | ☐ spelling | ☐ capitals to begin each line |
   | ☐ punctuation | ☐ capitals in the title |

   b.
☐ punctuation	☐ capitals to begin each line
☐ capitals in the title	☐ date in the heading
☐ topic sentences and supporting details	

2. Use the checklist you chose to help you edit this poem.

3. What do you think is the point of the poem? Is it just about the author's relationship with bees, or is she talking about something more?

0-7696-4057-5 *Proofreading and Editing*

Name _____   Date _____

Rhyme Schemes

Poems do not have to rhyme, but many do. Poems that do rhyme have identifiable rhyming patterns called **rhyme schemes.** The rhyme scheme is identified by using alphabet letters to identify the pairs of lines that rhyme. Sometimes these rhyming lines are together, and sometimes they are separate.

a   A timeless tree stood

b   On the edge of a dream

a   And thought that it could

b   Run like the stream.

Read the poems below and on page 72. Proofread them, and determine the rhyme scheme or pattern for each poem. On the short lines next to each line of each poem, write the letter for that part of the rhyme scheme. As you find a new type of rhyming sound, use the next letter in the alphabet to identify it.

Ballad of a Cherry Pie

_____ We met by yonder cherry tree.

_____ I glanced at Her, she winkd at me

_____ I oferred her a slice of pie.

_____ How could I know our love would die?

_____ After a bite, her watry eyes

_____ gazed at me; she gave a cry

_____ and gaged; she turned and ran away.

_____ I have not seen her since that day.

_____ You see, I like my pye with spice.

_____ Chili pouder tastes so nice!

_____ But my love I lost, so now I cry...

_____ Say, would you like a peice of pie!

by Norm Sneller

Rhyme Schemes (cont.)

Ode to Autumn

_____ Season of mists and mello fruitfulness!

_____ close bosom-friend of the maturing sun;

_____ Conspiring with him how to lode and bless

_____ With fruit the vines that round the thatch-eaves run;

_____ To bent with apples the moss'd cottage-trees,

_____ And fill all fruit with ripeness to the core;

_____ To swell the gourd, and plump the hazel shells

_____ with a sweat kernel; to set budding more,

_____ And still more, later flowers for the bees,

_____ Until they think warm days will never cease,

_____ For summer has o'er-brimmed their clammy cells.

by John Keats

0-7696-4057-5 _Proofreading and Editing_

Rhyme Schemes (cont.)

Editors must interpret the meaning of a poem. Read the following poem, and write the letters for its rhyme scheme on the lines next to the ends of each line of the poem. Then answer the questions that follow about the meaning of the poem.

Pebble Rings, Like Memories

_____ The old stone bridge across Rügen Bay

_____ Is one of my favorite places to play.

_____ I toss pebbles for Mom, and a pebble for Dad,

_____ And a rock for the horses and chickens we had.

_____ I watch as each of the stones makes rings

_____ Like the song that each of my memories sings.

_____ For my wife—for my dear and precious Lenore—

_____ My hands and my eyes throw several more.

_____ And then, before my playing is done

_____ I throw in the most important one,

_____ For the memory of my son.

1. Is the writer of the poem happy, or sad? How can you tell?

    _____

    _____

2. What do the pebbles the speaker is throwing symbolize?

    _____

    _____

3. Do you think that throwing the pebbles helps the speaker feel better about his losses, or makes him feel worse?

    _____

    _____

    _____

0-7696-4057-5 *Proofreading and Editing*

Revising:

Sentences

Colorful Words

A good editor must be able to revise as well as proofread and edit. Revising is not the same as editing. When one edits or proofreads, he or she finds and fixes mistakes in the writing. **Revision** makes the writing better, or more interesting. A few ways to revise are to choose more complex words, add details, and combine short sentences. One can also try to use more specific, colorful words.

First try: Carol looked at the clouds.

Revised: Carol viewed the fluffy white clouds against the pure blue sky, and imagined she saw amazing images in the shapes of the clouds.

First try: Bill was nervous about going to the principal's office.

Revised: Bill's heart pounded crazily in his chest as he worriedly walked the last few feet to the principal's office.

Revise the following sentences.

1. I enjoy tennis.

    _____

    _____

2. They went out to eat and had a nice meal.

    _____

    _____

3. Jackson liked the cake. He ate it quickly.

    _____

    _____

4. Shona was concerned about failing the class.

    _____

    _____

Out with Clichés

Revising:

Sentences

An editor checks to make sure that a writer does not use clichés or phrases that have been repeated so much that they have become worn-out. Using too many clichés the reader has heard before can make writing dull and uninteresting. Everyone knows what the phrase "blind as a bat" means, but it is better to use your own words. Sometimes clichés are difficult to explain or understand, especially if the reader does not know the cliché. An editor makes sure to change clichés to more original language, when editing a piece of writing.

Read the following sentences. Try to rewrite the sentence to mean the same thing, without using the underlined clichés.

1. Those donuts we got today really *hit the spot*.

   _____

2. The new outfit from that expensive store *cost me an arm and a leg*.

   _____

3. The facts of the case are so obvious that it should be *cut and dried* for the jurors to come to a verdict.

   _____

4. That baby is just *cute as a button*, and he's the *spitting image* of his father.

   _____

5. The inspector said it would be *as easy as pie* to find the suspect.

   _____

6. He's been working at two jobs and going to class, although it's not healthy to *burn the candle at both ends*.

   _____

7. Our dry cleaning methods are *tried and true*, so you can rely on our work.

   _____

8. In spite of weeks of planning and negotiation, the budget proposal was turned down, so the committee will have to go *back to the drawing board*.

   _____

0-7696-4057-5 *Proofreading and Editing*

Revising:

Sentences

Who Needs Help?

Editors check to see that the most effective word is used in a sentence. Active verbs tend to make sentences more interesting than passive verbs. An active verb describes someone doing something. A passive verb shows something being done to someone. Editors check to make sure the writer uses the most active verbs possible.

Active verb: Janice wrapped the package.

Passive verb: The package was wrapped by Janice.

Read the following sentences. You are the editor of this story about a busy shop. Can you make the language clearer for the reader by revising the sentences to be active instead of passive?

1. The counter *was lined with* busy shoppers looking at the display of jewelry, gloves, and scarves.

   _____

2. The woman wearing a green jacket *was asked by* Janice if she needed some help.

   _____

3. A reply *was quickly given* to Janice by the woman, "No thank you, I'm just looking."

   _____

4. A beautiful scarf *was being picked up and admired* by a woman in a brown dress.

   _____

5. She *was promptly asked by Janice,* "Do you need help?"

   _____

6. Janice *was told by the customer*, "No thank you, I'm just looking."

   _____

7. Janice finally decided to relax, since neither of the customers needed to *be helped by her*.

   _____

Improving Writing

Revising:

Paragraphs

Most writing can be improved. When proofreading a paragraph, make sure all the details agree with the topic sentence. Also, make sure all the sentences aren't written in the same way or aren't the same length. If a certain word is repeated many times, use synonyms to replace that word. If ideas seem too complicated, revise them so they are easier to understand. Make sure the sentences use active verbs. Take out anything that does not fit in the paragraph.

Read these paragraphs. Then revise to make them better and rewrite the corrected paragraphs on the lines provided. Use the back if necessary.

1. Packages arriving in the mail from relatives. The house was really full of secrets. What was up? One day I came home from school. When I walked in the house, everyone yelled," surprise"! My family is really whispering a lot, lately. I knew that they were planning a party, but I couldn't tell when it would happen. My mother had really been baking a lot more than usual. I am so happy to see all my favorite friends and relatives had come to my party. That was the best treat of all. I got several gifts I had really wanted.

   _____

   _____

   _____

   _____

2. It was 7 a.m. in the morning. He was tired, but got up. He delivered papers to his route before school that day. He looked out window, and wished he didn't have to go out in the rain, but the route had to be done before school. He sat down at his desk, pen in hand, ready to open his copy of the test. Everyone in his class was a little nervous about this math test. These questions were about exactly the material he had studied last night. Its had been a long morning, and he still hadn't even gone to school yet! He looked at the test. He started to feel more confident.

   _____

   _____

   _____

   _____

Revising:

Letters

On Vacation

Letters can be improved by revising them, too. Read the following friendly letter. Edit the letter for spelling and punctuation.

July 17 2005

Dear Mom and Dad

   I'm here in the holtel room. Thanks for letting me go on vacation with Jaime and her family. Its queit now, but it hasn't been very quiet all weak. we are having a great time? Between me, Jaime, and her too little brothers, theres plenty of noise around here. The amusement park is grate? Yesterday Jaimes parent's let us go on fiv different rides. They even let us go on that water ride I like so much. They even let us stay up an our later than usal becaues there were a good movie on cable last night. The water ride was great but I was soking wet after. We went rite back to the hotel and changed our clothes. Tommorrow we are planning to go to a very large petting zooo they have here. Tomorrow wi will have lunch at a place near the zoo. Every day we do something. We have fun every day. I'm look forward to seeing you next week. Even though I'm having such a good time.

Love

Gwen

Revise the letter to make it better. When you finish, fill in the following blank checklist and edit any mistakes in your revision.

_____

_____

_____

_____

_____

☐ _____

☐ _____

☐ _____

☐ _____

☐ _____

Charity Drive

Read the following friendly letter. Edit the letter for spelling and punctuation.

Dear Mr. Sampson,

This letter is to thank you for your company's generous donation to our charity drive for the Science Student of the Year Scholarship Fund. Because of your employee's generous contributions, as well as your corporations contribution, and the funds your employees collected from your clients, we will be able to create scholarships for at least too more students this year

The fundraising dinner dance you sponsored was a great success. The cake and cookie sale you promotd in your company's cafeteria was also great success. The success of these efforts will help us to help two more students this year, than we did last year.

In conclusion, we just want to thank you for your company's generosity in our charity drive for our scholarship fund. Me and my colleages had a wonderful time at the diner dance!

Take care!

Mr. Winters

Revise the letter to make it better. When you finish, fill in the following blank checklist and edit any mistakes in your revision.

_____

_____

_____

_____

_____

_____

- [ ] _____
- [ ] _____
- [ ] _____
- [ ] _____
- [ ] _____

Town Recycling

Revising a newspaper article is actually quite easy. The important information to look for is **who** did **what, where, when, why,** and **how.** These questions must all be answered for the reader, in order for the article to be effective.

Town Recycling

   Our town now requires all residents to recycle. This proposal was made a law last month. It took three hours for the council to agree on this law. Recycling containers are available to each household, free of charge. Any resident may stop by the Department of Sanitation office, and pick one up. They can do this Monday through Saturday, from 9 a.m. to 6 p.m. The recycling containers are green. Not everyone in the town was in favor of the recycling law, but it finally passed. You must bring some identification and a piece of mail that shows you are a town resident. You can also obtain instruction on the correct way to sort recyclable materials for collection at the Department of sanitation office. Collection day will be every Wednesday morning, except for holidays.

Revise this article on the lines below. Include only the important information about the project. Make the article interesting to the reader. Take out any repetitive phrases or sentences. Begin new paragraphs where needed.

_____

_____

_____

_____

_____

_____

_____

_____

_____

_____

_____

0-7696-4057-5 *Proofreading and Editing*

Little League Teams

When more than one person is interviewed for an article, it is important to make it clear to the reader which person is speaking. It is also important that quotation marks are used correctly, so that the reader is aware of when he or she is reading the words of someone being interviewed or the words of the writer.

Revise this article on the lines below, making sure to handle the issue of quotations correctly. Also, revise for any other problems you find in the article.

The new rules for choosing players for local Little League baseball teams are affecting many students in the area who are anxious for their teams to be organized before the new season starts. Jeff Blake, last year's most valuable player on the Spring Street Orioles, said, I would love to be on the Orioles again, and that's what I'm hoping for, but I'll do my best on any team. Coach Ben Carter of the Orioles says I'd like to have Jeff on the team again, and all the other great players from last year. For instance, Rebecca Miles was a fantastic pitcher for the Orioles. I'll have to find out more about the new age and league requirements. I'd love to play for Coach Carter again, says the award-winning player. He's obviously a great player and an asset to the team, according to all the coaches. Coach Tim Vendi of the Downtown White Sox team says he loves all his players, but it might be a good idea for teams to be more consistent in terms of the players' ages. My players had a fantastic season, but they might do better against teams that are closer to them in age and experiences. For instance, when we played against the Redwings, it was a disadvantage that all their players were a lot taller than ours were. Another issue being explored is the coed nature of the teams. Mostly it seems to have worked out well. Some people believe that teams should be separated by gender. But Coach Linda Chelton commented, I believe that athletes should compete against each other based on ability. That should be the main thing we look at when forming teams.

0-7696-4057-5 *Proofreading and Editing*

Revising:

Reports

Mealtime Manners

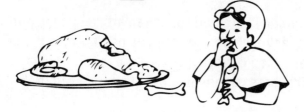

When you revise a report, make sure that all the topic sentences and supporting details fit together. Make sure the report is easy to understand. Use your sentence revision skills to remove any facts that are not needed in the report.

Read the first section of the report. Then follow the numbered instructions.

Today, most people in Western cultures expect to eat meals with their own silverware. Today, most people in Western cultures eat off their own plates. Some people like to share food in restaurants. Today, most people in Western cultures drink only from their own glasses at the dinner table.

1. One sentence in this paragraph does not support the main idea. Cross it out.

2. Most of the sentences in the above paragraph begin in the same way. Rewrite the paragraph, without the sentence you crossed out, in a way that keeps the reader interested.

_____

_____

_____

_____

_____

_____

_____

_____

Mealtime Manners (cont.)

Revising:

Reports

Read the next section of this report. Then follow the instructions.

Europeans did not always eat this way. In the sixteenth century, there were few mealtime rules of etiquette. Even members of the ruling classes rarely had their own plates and bowls. They ate sliced meat off the tip of the knife. Meat was a large part of the European diet. They would use shared spoons to eat soups. They would dip bread or their fingers into bowls of stew. There were not many different food options for dinner. Thought rude to eat something from a spoon someone else was being passed to. Chicken was prepared in a variety of recipes. If you had a chicken bone left in your hand, toss it under the table.

3. This paragraph has several sentences that do not support the main idea, and some poorly written sentences. Rewrite the paragraph on the lines below with the corrections/revisions.

_____

_____

_____

_____

_____

Read the next section of the report. Then follow the instructions.

While people in colonial America were still dipping their fingers into bowls of food, European royalty and nobility were starting to expand their tableware, and their table manners. The thought of sharing utensils was unsanitary and rude. By the eighteenth century, these new customs had spread to wealthy American settlers. As new landowners, they wanted to be as cool as and better than everyone else, even more than they would have been if they were in Great Britain.

4. One sentence of this paragraph is worded in a way that is inappropriate for the report. Rewrite the entire sentence to mean something similar in more appropriate language.

_____

_____

_____

_____

0-7696-4057-5 *Proofreading and Editing*

A Little Rain

Revising:

Narratives

When revising a narrative, it's important to make sure the writing keeps the reader's interest. Vary the types of sentences you use in the story. Also, change the length of the sentences so that they are not all the same.

Read the first section of the story. Then follow the instructions.

Jonathon sat on the bench. The sun was shining on him warmly. A slight breeze was blowing. "It's late again," Jonathon said to Grace, "but at least it's not raining." Almost on cue, a slight drizzle started to fall. Jonathon picked up his notebook and held it over his head. Grace did the same with a magazine. "Somewhere there are bus stops with shelters," said Grace, "but not around here."

1. The reader should be able to know the setting very soon in the story. The setting of this story is a bus stop near a high school, in a small town. Rewrite the story section so the setting is clearer to the reader. Remember to begin new paragraphs when someone speaks.

_____

_____

_____

_____

_____

_____

_____

_____

_____

A Little Rain (cont.)

Revising:

Narratives

Read the next section of the story. Then follow the instructions.

As it continued to drizzle, Jonathon and Grace were starting to get wet. "My good jacket is getting rained on," said Grace, "That's bad for a suede jacket." Their books were getting wet from the rain. It rained on Jonathon's notebook, and he got worried. "Oh, no!" he said, as he realized that some of his science report was sticking out of the notebook, being rained on. "Let's run into the coffee shop until this stops." said Grace. "We can't," said Jonathon, "the last time we did that we missed the bus when it came." So the two of them just huddled on the bench, having various possessions grow damp, and looking plaintively down the road for the bus. Suddenly they saw a welcome sight. The bus was coming. Just at the moment they stood up to get on the bus, the rain stopped, and the sun warmed them again. "Well that's ironic," said Grace.

2. A lot of ideas are repeated in this section. Take out the repetitive phrases, proofread, and rewrite the story to be clear and interesting.

    _____

    _____

    _____

    _____

    _____

    _____

    _____

Read the next section of the story. Then follow the instructions.

They got on the bus. They found some seats. They continued to talk. Grace asked about Jonathon's science report. He asked about her suede jacket. There was not as much damage as they thought.

3. Rewrite the sentences so that they vary in type and length.

    _____

    _____

    _____

    _____

    _____

Revising:

Poetry

Haiku

Although poetry is a creative form of writing, some forms of poetry have certain rules for their construction. For example, **haiku** is an ancient form of Japanese poetry that has rules for the length and number of lines. There should be three lines in each poem. The first line has five syllables, the second line has seven syllables, and the third line has five syllables.

Read the haiku poems below. Revise them so that they fit the construction rules of haiku.

1. In the lovely green pool a

   White lily floats on

   The sparkling water.

   _____

   _____

   _____

2. The life of spring

   Green plants budding new

   And blossoms flowing from fruit trees.

   _____

   _____

   _____

3. Steady in my walk

   My mind is free

   To wander off of the known path.

   _____

   _____

   _____

0-7696-4057-5 *Proofreading and Editing*

Success

Revising:

Poetry

Poetry is a creative form of writing, but a good editor may help revise a poem, so that the ideas of the poem are best expressed to the reader.

Read the poem below, and use your editing skills to make the ideas clearer to the reader. Rewrite the corrected/revised poem on the lines below.

Success

Many people want to know a successful meaning

But what? Is it?

Does it have to do with goals or prizes does it

Does it have to do with people getting

What people want the most in life

Is it working hard or not

working at all for what

you want to get or what you think you should have

Whatever.

it is, it is inside of you.

Right now!

_____

_____

_____

_____

_____

_____

_____

_____

_____

_____

_____

Name _____   Date _____

Now is the time to review all the proofreading skills you have learned throughout this book.

Read the following passage, and proofread for any spelling, punctuation, grammar, or other kinds of writing mistakes you might find.

For thousands of yeers, people has seen the northern lights multicolored rays of light streaking upward in the sky. Many native american tribes thought that the sight of the lites were an omen of something to come. Sum tribes thought that the lights was and oman of War, others thought they were humen spirits carrying torches to the sky. Europeans in the past have diffrent reacts to the northern lights. In 37 AD, a group of people in Ostia, italy, thought that the town was on fire when they saw the lights. In 1583, people in France believed superstitiously that the lights wer an omen of the end of the world. The northern lights have a science name, aura borealis. They are solar powered? The clouds of these particles is called plasma. The stream of plasma travling from the sun is calld solar wind. When the Solar wind disturbs the earth's magnetic field, the particles glow and create the aurora borealis. These lights, though beautiful, can create many problems because of the grate amount of energy they use. One display can use as much energie as it used by the entire population of the United States in a day. The charged particle bounce around the planets' magnetic field and cause atmospheric disturbances. Compasses point the wrong way, communications system's can be disrupted, and power systems can go out. The aurora borealis sometimes lights up the sky with bands of pink red green and blue rays of light. Newscasters and weather people usually report when the Northern lights are performing. Try to cach this information so you wont miss the show.

What You've Learned

Proofreading Team

Write two paragraphs about the best day you ever had at school. Write about what made that experience good and everything you remember about it. Include as many details as possible. Make two copies. Proofread and edit your mistakes on one copy. Then give the other copy to a classmate to proofread and edit. Have your partner give you his or her paper so that you can edit it. Afterwards, compare both copies of both compositions. Did each proofreading teammate find mistakes that the writer missed? Did it help to have someone else read your paper? What did you learn from this exercise?

Your Most Common Error

If you have any kind of career, what would it be? Write a one- to two-page story about a typical day in the career you would like to have. It could be anything at all. After you have written the story, proofread for mistakes with one of the checklists you have used. Write how many times you found errors for each of the items on the list. What was your most common mistake? Now you can be more careful about looking for that type of error in your writing.

Reading Aloud

It may help the editing process to read your paper aloud while you are correcting it. Write two separate paragraphs on important people in history. Choose two people from history whom you find particularly interesting. Write a paragraph about each person. After you write each paragraph, read one aloud. Then read the other silently. When you finish, switch the way you read each one and read them again. Did you mark more errors when you switched your way of reading?

Be the Reader

There is one more thing that might help you edit: pretend you are the reader. This means you will have to distance yourself from the text. Write a short paragraph on any topic you choose. Edit it. Then do something else for at least an hour. Come back to the piece later and reread it. Do you see anything that you would edit or rewrite the second time around? This strategy can help you be an even better editor than before.

Answer Key

Scoundrels on the Seas ....Page 5

1. seventeenth
2. merciless
3. Tew
4. captains
5. Captain
6. However,
7. Blackbeard
8. plank
9. One of the most
10. a captain

Aliens and New Worlds ....Page 6

1. Rice, 2
2. He, 1
3. Farm, 3
4. British, 2
5. Madeleine, 2
6. Martians, 2
7. Mars, 2
8. Some, 1
9. Guin, 2
10. War, 3

War Presidents ....Pages 7–8

1. When President Abraham Lincoln took office, the country was ready for war.
2. Abraham Lincoln was a president that believed in peace across the United States.
3. During his four short years in office, the president guided the country through the Civil War until the southern General Robert Lee surrendered in 1865.
4. Only fifty years later, President Woodrow Wilson stated that "the world must be safe for democracy" as he led the United States in World War I.
5. The United States had only twenty years of peace before Franklin Roosevelt was president and led the country through another World War in 1941.
6. c
7. a
8. c
9. c
10. a

Sunken History ....Page 9

Paragraphs should be edited according to rules.

A Space Station Mission ....Page 10

1. period
2. period
3. question mark
4. exclamation mark
5. period
6. period

Paragraph should be edited for punctuation.

Winter Vacation ....Page 11

Commas should be placed after the following words:
1st paragraph: We were in school, say, sky
2nd paragraph: At home, somewhere in the house, with our names on them, Out in the kitchen, Saturday, grandparents, aunts, uncles
3rd paragraph: On Friday, This was ironic

4th paragraph: down the green stairwell, Lazy

Performing Well ....Pages 12–13

1. couch;
2. dessert:
3. teachers: math department; history department;
4. (noun):
5. student;
6. museum;

Corrected sentences:
7. Ed wants to pursue lots of interests: biking, skating, and swimming.
8. I don't watch French movies without subtitles; I don't know enough French yet to understand.
9. My brother's favorite sport is basketball; baseball is the game I love.
10. There is one way to deal with this problem: be honest.

Family Tree ....Page 14

Story should be edited for quotation marks.

It Adds Up ....Page 15

1. She'll
2. He'd
3. He's
4. I'm
5. You're
6. they're
7. we're
8. he'd

Own It! ....Page 16

1. our teacher's idea
2. students' observations
3. forest animals' reactions to humans
4. plant's leaves and roots
5. forest's soil
6. bluebird's wings
7. soil's texture
8. beetle's legs

Dog Data ....Page 17

1. friend?
2. delete the semicolon
3. ancestor.
4. Unlike a wolf's bark, a dog's bark is rather noisy.
5. When a barks, he is saying "I notice something unusual. Pay attention!"
6. A barking dog wants one thing: your attention.
7. The expression "wolf down one's food," comes from observing wolves' quick eating habits.

A Love of Theatre ....Page 18

Edit paragraph for correct italics.

Answer Key

In the Village ....Page 19

Have you ever wondered what a typical Incan farming village was like?
Picture this: huge . . .
Put periods and commas in appropriate places.
Put words *adobe*, *chicha*, and *chasqui* in italics.
They are happy to see him; he is their only source of news.

Expert Spelling ....Page 20

1. access
2. estimate
3. feasted
4. speak
5. terrible
6. greatest
7. generous
8. table
9. fry
10. goodbye
11. independent
12. cooperation
13. bigger
14. dirty
15. pretense

Remarkable Rooms ....Page 21

overnite, change to overnight
loonie, change to loony
ancored, change to anchored
convertid, change to converted
nesesities, change to necessities
acktualy, change to actually
apeal, change to appeal
spatious, change to spacious
reeched, change to reached
piranas, change to pirhanas
entertane, change to entertain
capsal, change to capsule
resembel, change to resemble
mashines, change to machines
entirley, change to entirely
soled, change to solid
acommodation, change to accommodation

Family Reunion ....Page 22

1. cousins
2. aunt's, brothers
3. brothers'
4. children's
5. relatives', it's
6. cousins'
7. mom's, family's
8. its

Home Décor ....Page 23

Answers may vary. Edit each sentence for correct use of active verbs.

Surprise! ....Pages 25–26

The following questions should be circled: 1, 2, 5, 6, 7, 10, 11, 12, and 15.

16. happened
17. told
22. pulled
23. said
18. picked
19. wondered
20. said
21. asked
24. struggled
25. screamed
26. smiled

Class Project ....Page 27–29

1. Our class decided to do a project together, because we like working together.
2. When many people cooperate on something, they usually get a great result.
3. My friend Mark suggested we do a video about the historical society in our town, and about its origins, because it interests him so much.
4. I heard that one of the students promised to bring in a video camera from home, but ("he," or "she," or "he or she") couldn't bring it, after all.
5. Jennelle wrote a script and so did Kayla, and we could see ("Jennelle" or "Kayla") was very talented.
6. Keith and Jay created a videotaping schedule, and made copies of the script, and ("Keith" or "Jay") handed ("schedules" or "copies of the script," or "both") out to all the students in the class.
7. Our teacher took us on many trips to the historical society, and we found it to be a very interesting place.
8. The members of our class found out that their town had been founded by James Peterson, and Robert Stevens, and ("James Peterson" or "Robert Stevens") was a very interesting person who invented several things.

School Uniforms ....Pages 30–31

1. In my school, we all wear school uniforms.
2. Our uniform consists of a white shirt, a gray jacket, and blue pants, and everyone cleans his or her own uniform.
3. A funny thing happened recently to my friends and me on the boys' basketball team.
4. We visited the players at another school, to play basketball with them.
5. Our school bus driver was late in getting us there, because he (or she) couldn't find a route without traffic.
6. When we got to the locker room, the team and I had to change into our basketball uniforms very quickly.
7. We left our school uniforms all over the place; in fact, my friend William threw his jacket at me in a panic.
8. Our team won, and we all felt pretty good.
9. But when we went back to the locker room, we could see we had a problem.
10. The school uniforms were scattered all over the floor; it was a mess.

0-7696-4057-5 *Proofreading and Editing*

Answer Key

11. Since the parts are identical, it wasn't easy for us to figure out which parts belonged to each one of us.
12. Was this grey jacket mine or his? Should I put on that shirt, or hand it to him?
13. It took a long while, but we finally sorted out the clothes, and each person had his own uniform back.
14. Of course, on the bus trip home, I found a note in my jacket pocket that said, "Remember to bring home your science book," in someone else's handwriting.
15. I waved the note in the air, and William and I realized we had each other's jackets.
16. "Thanks a lot" said William glumly, "Now I have no excuse to forget bringing home my science book."

A Day at the Beach ....Page 32

1. My friends and I are the kind of people (who or that) really like going to the beach.
2. It rained for ten days in a row, which meant we could not go to the beach.
3. One morning I woke up and saw it was the kind of day that was perfect for going to the beach.
4. It's Jenny's mom who always drives us to the beach when no one else can.
5. She's really the kind of person (who or that) who likes to help out in a pinch.
6. After Jenny and her mom picked me up, it was Dennis who was to be picked up.
7. He had on a funny looking hat, which made us laugh.
8. "Laugh all you want," said Dennis, "but I'm the kind of person (who or that) burns easily."
9. We set up our things on the sand, and sat under a sun that was extremely hot.
10. It was a day that was filled with a lot of fun.
11. Of course, Dennis had the last laugh. By the time we went home, he was the only one who didn't have a sunburned face!

Contemplating Color ....Page 33

1. It seems that blue is the calmest color of all of the colors in the rainbow.
2. Blue has often been chosen as the most relaxing color, symbolizing tranquility.
3. Red makes people feel more excited than other colors do, since it increases heart rate and speeds up breathing.
4. For centuries, the color purple was the favorite of kings and queens. That was originally because purple dye was the most expensive, and only the richest of all people could afford it.

Venice.......................Page 34

1. Just before we left on this trip, a television was delivered to our house.
2. A man drove it in a van to our house to deliver it.
3. Today, in Venice, I watched a family bring home a new TV to their house in a very different way.
4. Because the family lived on a canal, the set had to be transported by rowboat.
5. People live in the strangely beautiful Venice, because of the city's wonderful surprises and canals.
6. The canals are full of *gondolas*, large canoes that serve as taxis, run by boat operators.
7. People also may travel on a faster and more efficient *vaporetto*, which goes quickly from station to station.
8. Venice was first built 1,000 years ago, on a series of 118 islands that filled the Lagoon of Venice.

One Negative Is Enough.......................Page 35
Sentences should be edited for double negatives.

When Lightning Strikes ....Page 36

1. CX
2. S
3. C
4. C
5. CX
6. S
7. Lightning rods are still in use today, and they are especially handy in places like Florida, which have many storms.
8. Many people think lightning is just a dangerous phenomenon, but lightning returns negative energy to the earth, which produces nitrogen that plants need to grow.

Speak the Language ....Pages 37–38

1. S		6. S
2. C		7. S
3. C		8. S
4. C		9. c
5. S		10. b

Paragraph should be edited for sentence structure.

London in 1601 ....page 39

1. S		5. F
2. F		6. S
3. S		7. F
4. F		8. S

Jessica's Activities ....Page 40

1. c

Answer Key

2. a
3. b & c

Doctor Anna ....Page 41
1. b   3. a
2. c   4. b

Canoes ....Page 42
1. c
2. a

When the Chips Are Down ....Pages 43–44
Edit for punctuation and indentation.

High Tech Tale ....Page 45
a. 1   f. 5
b. 2   g. 3
c. 7   h. 8
d. 10   i. 4
e. 6   j. 9

At Sheila's House ....Page 46
A new paragraph should begin each time a new person speaks.

Mathew Brady's Career ....Page 47
Order of paragraphs:
1, 4, 3, 2, and 5.

Tell All about It ....Page 48
1. a   4. c
2. a   5–6. Answers will vary.
3. b

Pick a Purpose ....Page 49
1. a   4. c
2. a   5. b
3. c

A Famous Composer ....Pages 50–51
1. a   5. c
2. b   6. b
3. c   7. c
4. b

Simplicity ....Pages 52–53
1–4. Revisions may vary.
5. a
6. b

Dinner in a Restaurant ....Page 54
Edit conversation for correct use of homophones.

Check the Source ....Page 55
1. a   4. b
2. a   5. Encyclopedia, book, etc.
3. c

Benjamin Franklin ....Pages 56–57
1. d
2. Paragraphs should be edited with proofreading marks.
3. Suggestions include the Internet, a biography book about Benjamin Franklin, and the encyclopedia.
4. Internet article

Checking the List ....Pages 58–59
1. a, b, c, f, h, i   4. a
2. a, d   5. all
3. a, c

The sentences should be revised as follows:

Where can you find 100 million year old dinosaur blood? One can find it in amber, a substance known more for its decorative uses than for its scientific value; that is, until recently.

Amber is actually hardened tree resin that has been fossilized. Most of it is mined in the Baltic Sea area. It is smooth and warms quickly to the touch. The ancient Greeks called it "electron" perhaps because amber builds up a small, negative charge when it is rubbed.

In the 1700s, an entire room of 100,000 carved amber pieces was given as a gift to Tsar Peter the Great of Russia. This golden room, lit by more than 500 candles, was said to be dazzling in its beauty.

Editing Letters ....Page 60–61
Letters should be edited according to checklist.
1. d
2. c

Life in Yakutia ....Pages 62–63
1. Yakutia in northern Russia is a naturally cold place.
2. Answers will vary.
3. Report should be edited according to checklist.
4. Photo of a house in Yakutsk
5. to verify correct use of words

Unscrambling Script ....Pages 64–65
1. c
2. Report should be edited for accuracy in content.
3. d.
4. Report should be edited according to checklist.

The Baseball Card ....Pages 66–67
1. Report should be edited according to checklist.
2. 3rd person

3. How does the man get money?
4. Answers may vary.

Geraldo's Journal.....................Pages 68–69

1. Answers may vary
2. b
3. being lost at sea
4. yes, they reached land
5. a
6. Story should be edited according to checklist.

The Bee Is Not Afraid of Me.....................Page 70

1. a
2. Poem should be edited according to the first checklist.
3. Answers may vary.

Rhyme Schemes.....................Pages 71–73

Ballad of a Cherry Pie
a a b b b b a a c c b b

Ode to Autumn
a b a b c d e d c c e

Pebble Rings, Like Memories
a a b b c c d d e e e

1. The poem uses words like "play" and "song" that seem happy, but the writer is remembering something sad.
2. The pebbles symbolize memories of people who are gone.
3. Throwing pebbles seems to make the speaker feel better.

Colorful Words.....................Page 74

1–4. Revisions may vary.

Out with Clichés.....................Page 75

1–8. Revisions may vary. Students should use more interesting ways of expression that do not involve any clichés.

Who Needs Help?.....................Page 76

1. Busy shoppers lined the counter, looking at the display of jewelry, gloves, and scarves.
2. Janice asked the woman wearing a green jacket if she needed some help.
3. The woman quickly gave a reply to Janice by the woman, "No thank you, I'm just looking."
4. A woman in a brown dress picked up and admired s beautiful scarf.
5. Janice promptly asked her, "Do you need help?"
6. The customer told Janice, "No thank you, I'm just looking."
7. Janice finally decided to relax, since neither of the customers needed her to help them.

Improving Writing.....................Page 77

Revisions may vary; some sentences must be rearranged for the purposes of correct sequences. Sentence fragments and grammar must be corrected, and words that have been repeated too many times should be removed. Here are suggested revisions:

1. Packages were arriving in the mail from relatives. My family had been whispering a lot, lately, and the house seemed to be full of secrets. My mother had been baking a lot more than usual. I wondered what was going on. I knew that they were planning a party, but I couldn't tell when it would happen.
   One day I came home from school. When I walked in the house, everyone yelled," Surprise!" I got several gifts I had really wanted, but I was happy to see all my favorite friends and relatives had come to my party. That was the best treat of all.

2. It was 7 a.m. in the morning. He was tired, but he got up. He looked out window, and wished he didn't have to go out in the rain, but the route had to be done before school. He delivered papers to his route before school that day. It had been a long morning, and he still hadn't even gone to school yet!
   When he got to school, he sat down at his desk, pen in hand, ready to open his copy of the test. Everyone in his class was a little nervous about this math test. He looked at the test. These questions were about exactly the material he had studied last night! He started to feel more confident.

Charity Drive.....................Page 79

Letter should be corrected for punctuation and grammar. Some revisions should also be made.

Town Recycling.....................Page 80

Revisions will vary.

Little League Teams.....................Page 81

Here is a suggested revision:
   The new rules for choosing players for local Little League baseball teams are affecting many students in the area who are anxious for their teams to be organized before the new season starts.
   Jeff Blake, last year's most valuable player on the Spring Street Orioles, said "I would love to be on the Orioles again, and that's what I'm hoping for, but I'll do

Answer Key

my best on any team."

Coach Ben Carter of the Orioles says, "I'd like to have Jeff on the team again, and all the other great players from last year. I'll have to find out more about the new age and league requirements."

"I'd love to play for Coach Carter again, says the award-winning player."

He's obviously a great player and an asset to the team, according to all the coaches.

Coach Tim Vendi of the Downtown White Sox team says he loves all his players, but it might be a good idea for teams to be more consistent in terms of the players' ages. "My players had a fantastic season," says Vendi, "but they might do better against teams that are closer to them in age and experiences. For instance, when we played against the Redwings, it was a disadvantage that all their players were a lot taller than ours were."

Another issue being explored is the coed nature of the teams. Mostly it seems to have worked out well. For instance, Rebecca Miles was a fantastic pitcher for the Orioles.

Some people believe that teams should be separated by gender. But Coach Linda Chelton commented, "I believe that athletes should compete against each other based on ability. That should be the main thing we look at when forming teams."

Mealtime Manners.............................Pages 82–83

1. Cross out: Some people like to share food in restaurants.
2. Revisions may vary. Students should be changing the phrase, "Today, most people . . ."
3. Cross out these sentences: Meat was a large part of the European diet. There were not many different food options for dinner. Chicken was prepared in a variety of recipes. Revisions may vary.
4. This sentence should be rewritten: As new landowners, they wanted to be as cool as and better than everyone else is, as they would have been if they were in Great Britain.

A Little Rain..Pages 84–85

1. Revisions may vary. Students should make the setting clear early in the paragraph, also make quotes start new paragraphs.
2. Revisions may vary. Students should paraphrase so that there are no so many "rained on" phrases.
3. Revisions may vary. Combine or add to some sentences to make them more interesting.

Haiku ....Page 86

1. In the lovely green
Pool a white lily floats on
The sparkling water.
2. The life of spring green
Plants budding new and blossoms
Flowing from fruit trees.
3. Steady in my walk
My mind is free to wander
Off of the known path.

Success ....Page 87

Revisions may vary. Here is one suggestion:
Many people want to know the meaning of success,
But what is it?
Does it have to do with goals or prizes?
Does it have to do with what people want the most in life?
Is it working hard or not working at all?
Is it getting what you want to get or what you think you should have?
Whatever it is, it is inside of you, right now!

Northern Lights..Page 88

Report should be edited for grammar, spelling, punctuation, etc.

0-7696-4057-5 *Proofreading and Editing*

Proofreading Marks

Capitalize a letter: w̳

bi̲lbo ba̲ggins

Lowercase a letter: ø⃥ *lc*

H̸ouse   *lc*

Delete a letter or a word: ⸜

the ~~the~~ big ogre

Change the order of letters or words: ↻

reci̲e̲ve

Add a word, a period, a comma or other punctuation: ∧ ˝ �

The Lord ^of^ *the Rings*

Show start of a new paragraph: ¶

That's why I really like astronomy. ¶Another favorite pasttime I have is studying dinosaurs. My collection of dinosaur resources includes several books, models, and a real fossil I found while visiting Arizona.

0-7696-4057-5 *Proofreading and Editing*